JOSHUA

THROUGH

RUTH

WESLEY BIBLE STUDIES

wesleyan
PUBLISHING HOUSE
wphstore.com

CONTENTS

INTRODUCTION

God's Faithfulness to All Generations

According to a 2009 PEW research poll of nearly three thousand people, about two-thirds of the people sixty-five years and older said religion is very important to them. Just over half of those age thirty to forty-nine agreed with the older generation, and only 44 percent of people age eighteen to twenty-nine said religion is very important to them. Apparently, the gap between each generation is not restricted to the younger's uncanny ability to catch on quickly to every advance in technology. Nevertheless, God's patience and mercy span all generations.

FROM JOSHUA TO THE TIMES OF THE JUDGES

When God appointed Joshua to succeed Moses as Israel's leader, He told him to be strong and courageous and to obey His Word. He promised to be with Joshua and deliver the Promised Land into his hand. Joshua lived up to the charge he received from God, and God faithfully granted Joshua the Promised Land. The book of Joshua reports an occasional defeat, but for the most part it spotlights Israel's victories under Joshua's leadership. As you study the book of Joshua, you will be impressed with Joshua's courage and faith and with God's faithfulness to the generation that followed Joshua into the Promised Land. You will also find yourself saying "Amen" often as you read Joshua's farewell address to the nation and his personal testimony: "As for me and my household, we will serve the LORD" (Josh. 24:15).

And you will applaud his boldness at commanding the Israelites to "throw away the foreign gods that are among you and yield your hearts to the LORD, the God of Israel" (v. 23).

Yes, that first generation to live in Canaan had held on to foreign gods. Yet God remained faithful to His people—and ever patient with them!

THE TIMES OF THE JUDGES

The next generation precipitated a downward spiral away from the Lord. The times of the judges include, but are not limited to, the books of Judges and Ruth. During this period, each generation did what was right in its own eyes (Judg. 17:6; 21:25), which means it did what was wrong in the Lord's eyes.

You will observe an oft-repeated cycle as you study Judges. The Israelites' sin brought divine judgment in the form of an oppressor; the people repented and cried out for deliverance; God appointed a judge to deliver His people; and peace ensued until the people fell into sin again. It is a sorry history, but God's faithfulness throughout that period shines like a diamond against a black background.

The brief book of Ruth further highlights God's faithfulness and shows how Ruth, a Gentile woman, came to believe in the God of Israel. And even more amazing, she became an ancestress to the Messiah.

The writer of Psalm 89 pledged to sing of the Lord's great love forever and to make His faithfulness known to all generations (v. 1). Let your study inspire you to follow the psalmist's example.

GOD CHOOSES A LEADER

Joshua 1:1–17

God chooses to do a great work through a surrendered leader.

God called and equipped Moses, a man of great faith, to lead His people from Egypt to the Promised Land. After Moses died, a new leader was needed. So God appointed Joshua, who had been Moses' assistant. Joshua, too, was a man of faith who would heed God's Word.

This study shows us that God appoints godly leaders to guide His people at specific times and for specific purposes. We should thank God for past leaders and cooperate with those He has appointed to lead us now.

COMMENTARY

The book of Joshua divides into three main sections: (1) the entrance into (chs. 1–5) and conquest of (chs. 6–12) the land; (2) the apportioning and division of the land (chs. 13–21), and (3) three different events once the people were in the land (chs. 22–24).

The first chapter of Joshua recounts Joshua's commissioning as leader and establishes the theological paradigm through which the entrance into and conquest of the land are to be understood.

Joshua was first introduced in the Pentateuch. There he was shown to be a military leader in the battle against the Amalekites (Ex. 17:8–14). He was Moses' assistant (that is, leader-in-training; Num. 11:28), present with Moses on Mount Sinai (Ex. 24:12–13; 32:17) and when Moses went into the Tent of Meeting (Ex. 33:11).

He was one of the twelve spies sent into the land in Numbers 13–14 (compare Num. 26:65; 32:12).

Near the end of the Pentateuch, Joshua was appointed as Moses' successor (Num. 27:15–23; 34:17; Deut. 1:38; 3:18–22, 28; 31:1–23; 34:9). Given those previous passages in the Pentateuch, Joshua 1 must be seen as a reaffirmation of Joshua's leadership to which he had already been both divinely designated and publicly commissioned, prior to Moses' death.

The repeated mention of Moses in chapter 1 (eleven times) drew a correlation between the two leaders and their tasks so that Joshua's leadership was seen in a comparable light to that of Moses' leadership. The Lord assured Joshua of His presence in the same way He was with Moses (v. 5; compare v. 17). That promise echoed the Lord's declaration to Moses at his calling in Exodus 3:12: "I will be with you." Also, the people reassured Joshua of their obedience based on that given to Moses in verse 17.

WORDS FROM WESLEY

Joshua 1:1

The servant of the Lord—This title is given to Moses here and ver. 2 as also Deuteronomy 34:5, and is repeated not without cause, to reflect honour upon him, to give authority to his laws and writings, in publishing whereof he acted as God's servant, in His name: and that the Israelites might not think of Moses above what was meet, remembering that he was not the Lord himself, but only the Lord's servant; and therefore not to be too pertinaciously followed in all his institutions, when the Lord himself should come and abolish part of the Mosaical dispensation; it being but reasonable that he who was only a servant in God's house, should give place to Him who was the Son, and heir, and Lord of it. (ENOT)

First Speech: The Lord's Commissioning of Joshua (Josh. 1:1–9)

The Lord's speech to Joshua was an installation speech, the key component of which is the commissioning of the person to the task the new leadership position entails. The literary form of this type of speech is composed of four common elements.

A Statement of the Task. For Joshua, the task was to lead the people across the Jordan River into the land, to take possession of the land, and to allot it to them as an inheritance (**get ready to cross the Jordan River into the land** [v. 2]; **you will lead these people to inherit the land** [v. 6]).

WORDS FROM WESLEY

Joshua 1:2

Now therefore arise—Let not the withering of the most useful hands be the weakening of ours. When God has work to do, He will either find or make instruments fit to carry it on. Moses the servant is dead; but God the master is not: He lives forever. (ENOT)

An Exhortation of Encouragement. Such exhortations are expressed positively as "be strong, be courageous" or conversely through "do not be afraid." Here that command was repeated three times. **Be strong and courageous. . . . Be strong and very courageous. . . . Be strong and courageous** (vv. 6–7, 9). **Do not be terrified; do not be discouraged** (v. 9), shows its centrality in the message. The exhortation was also repeated in the fourth speech in verse 18 as the people exhorted Joshua, "Only be strong and courageous!"

In this speech, the exhortation is tied specifically to all the other elements. In verse 6, it is linked with the statement of the task of leading the people to inherit the land, and in verse 7, it transitions into the command to be obedient to the law (compare also Josh. 23:6). Thus Joshua was to display resoluteness with respect to both his military leadership of the people and his personal devotion to doing God's will, out of which his spiritual leadership would arise.

In Joshua 1:9, the exhortation is linked to the promise of the divine presence in such a way that the latter provides the basis as to why Joshua could be strong. In other words, Joshua could be courageous *because* he had the assurance that God was with him, enabling and empowering him. Thus the exhortation must be understood as a call to exercise faith and trust in God's promise rather than being merely a summoning up of one's own inner fortitude, courage, and valor.

An Affirmation of Assurance of the Divine Presence and Help. Such occurs in two ways in this type of speech. The first was through the specific phraseing of "the LORD being with" the person. Twice in this speech the Lord reassured Joshua, **"I will be with you"** (v. 5; see also v. 9). In verse 5, it is further reinforced through **"I will never leave you nor forsake you."** This assurance was also expressed in the fourth speech by the people to Joshua in verse 17 ("Only may the LORD your God be with you") as they too acknowledged that a key quality needed by the leader was the divine presence.

That promise of the divine presence did not simply mean the person would in some nebulous way sense God's surrounding presence. Rather, it was a powerful promise of the Lord's abiding with the person specifically to strengthen him or her for the task to which the Lord had called the person. (See Jesus' similar promise in Matt. 28:19–20 to us, His followers, as we are commissioned to carry out the task of making disciples throughout the world.)

The second affirmation came in declarations that the Lord would fight for them or give them victory. Such assurances of victory are expressed in verses 2–3 (**the land I am about to give to them. . . . I will give you every place where you set your foot**) and verse 5 (**No one will be able to stand up against you**).

An Exhortation to Keep the Law. This becomes a condition for the successful fulfilling of the task. In verses 7–8, the Lord commanded Joshua to be fully observant of the law. The specific designation of the **Book of the Law** (v. 8) probably referred to the portions of the book of Deuteronomy written by Moses as mentioned in Deuteronomy 31:9, 24–26.

This command was emphasized through five repeated phrases, with the similar phrases **be careful to obey all the law** (Josh 1:7) and **be careful to do everything written in it** (v. 8) beginning and concluding the section. The first two phrases in verse 7 (**Be careful to obey all the law** and **do not turn from it to the right or to the left**) are synonymous and stress complete obedience, without deviating from the law in any way. The first two phrases in verse 8 (**Do not let this Book of the Law depart from your mouth** and **meditate on it day and night**) are probably to be understood in a more contrastive manner. They stress the dual aspect of publicly speaking forth the law to the people and personally taking it in.

WORDS FROM WESLEY

Joshua 1:8

Out of thy mouth—That is, thou shalt constantly read it, and upon occasion on discourse of it, and the sentence which shall come out of thy mouth, shall in all things be given according to this rule. *Day and night*—That is, diligently study, and upon all occasions consider what is God's will and thy duty. The greatness of thy place and employments shall not hinder thee from this work, because this is the only rule of all thy private actions, and public administrations. (ENOT)

The reason for being observant of the law was so that Joshua would have success (**that you may be successful wherever you go** [v. 7]; **then you will be prosperous and successful** [v. 8]).

The promise of prosperity and success in the context of this type of commissioning speech was not to be understood as a generic, blanket statement that the person would receive manifold material blessings and wealth in the various vicissitudes of life, but was rather tied to the particular task to which God was calling the person. Thus it was a specific promise assuring the success of the specific venture, which in this case was the conquest of the land.

The repeated emphasis on obeying God's law stressed both the spiritual quality necessary for effective leadership (obedience to God) and the source of that spiritual direction (the law of God). Thus, the key to Joshua's carrying out his leadership role and the successful completion of the commissioned task was not his leadership abilities or his military strategies, but rather his unswerving spiritual commitment to obeying the commands of God.

Although delineating the specific task that was to be undertaken, the key persuasive purpose of this type of speech was to give the one commissioned the sense of assurance that the task, regardless of how difficult it was, could nevertheless be carried out because of the divine presence that was there to enable the successful completion. So here, the Lord was trying to encourage Joshua as he assumed the leadership position passed down from Moses, which carried with it the daunting task and responsibility of leading the people to take possession of the land.

Second Speech: Joshua's Commands to the People (Josh. 1:10–11)

In the second (vv. 10–11) and third (vv. 12–15) speeches, Joshua transmitted the divine orders to the appropriate people. In verses 10–11, he gave orders to the **officers of the people** (the tribal leaders who performed military as well as civil and judicial duties). In verse 2, God had told Joshua to "get ready to cross the Jordan River into the land I am about to give to them—to the Israelites." Verses 10–11 suggest the immediate implementation of that divine command, as Joshua communicated almost verbatim the divine command and promise to the people: **Get your supplies ready. Three days from now you will cross the Jordan here to go in and take possession of the land the LORD your God is giving you** (v. 11).

The time reference of **three days from now** did not mean "after three days," but rather "the day after tomorrow." The Hebrew idiom included both the current day and the day of the event. The immediacy of Joshua's implementing the divine command was evident, with only enough delay to allow time for the necessary preparations.

Third Speech: Joshua's Commands to the Tribes (Josh. 1:12–15)

In verses 12–15, Joshua reminded the two and a half tribes of the command given to them by Moses (Num. 32:2–32; Deut. 3:18–20). The Lord had given the tribes of Reuben, Gad, and the half-tribe of Manasseh permission to settle and occupy the Transjordan territory captured by the Israelites, with the proviso that they accompany the other tribes across the Jordan to fight with them in taking possession of their land. The conquest of the Promised Land was to be a united effort by *all* the tribes taking possession of *all* the territory.

In Joshua 1:14, for the first time in the chapter, the command indicates the military nature of the venture: **all your fighting men, fully armed** (or, in battle array) **must cross over**. Also, the language of verse 15—**taken possession**—connotes that such was done by force; it involved the dispossessing of those currently occupying the land. Although they must fight to take the land, the ultimate goal was God giving **rest** (vv. 13, 15). **Rest** in this context meant the cessation of fighting due to the subjugation of the enemies (compare Deut. 12:10; 25:19; Josh. 21:44; 23:1).

Fourth Speech: Pledge of Obedience by the People (Josh. 1:16–17)

The main point of the fourth speech was the tribes' pledge of full obedience to Joshua and by implication to God's commands. Although the people pledged complete obedience, one cannot help but read their declaration with a sense of irony. They pledged obedience to Joshua in the same way they were obedient to Moses (**Just as we fully obeyed Moses, so we will obey you** [v. 17]). But the Pentateuch repeatedly characterizes the people as not being obedient to Moses! Also, this pledge of loyalty must be read in light of the Lord's and Moses' expectation that this new generation would not be faithful once they were in the land (Deut. 31:14–18, 24–29). Thus the rebellious, stubborn, and obnoxious qualities of the people in relationship to leadership raised the question as to whether the people would completely obey all that Joshua commanded them or be "faithful" to Joshua's commands similar to the way they were "faithful" to those of Moses.

●

WORDS FROM WESLEY

Joshua 1:16

And they answered—Not the two tribes and an half only, but the officers of all the people, in their name, concurring with the divine appointment, by which Joshua was set over them. Thus must we swear allegiance to our Lord Jesus, as the captain of our salvation. (ENOT)

DISCUSSION

When a company needs a new CEO, it may hire someone from outside the company or it may promote from within, as Moses did.

1. Read Exodus 17:13; 24:13; Numbers 14:30, 38; and Deuteronomy 34:9. What do these verses reveal about Joshua's character and credentials?

2. Based on Joshua 1:2–9, what would you say Joshua's job description included?

3. Compare Joshua 1:5 and Hebrews 13:5. How does assurance of the Lord's presence enable you to accept challenges?

4. Why do you think your spiritual leaders need to be strong and courageous?

5. How has the practice of obeying and meditating on God's Word helped you lead a successful life?

6. Read Numbers 32:25–32 and Deuteronomy 3:12–20. What were the Reubenites, the Gadites, and the half-tribe of Manasseh obligated to do before occupying their own land?

7. Why is unity so important to the success of a church?

8. Specifically, what help will you give your Christian brothers and sisters in the ongoing battle against the Devil and his forces?

PRAYER

Father, thank You for Your promise to be with us when we faithfully answer Your call. Thank You for those who support us. Help us to obey all You command, completely, and to step forward fearlessly, marching toward success.

BREAKING DOWN WALLS

Joshua 2:1–14, 17–21

Faith breaks down the walls between people.

If a poor man wearing unwashed, tattered clothes wandered into the average church service, would he receive a loving welcome? More than a few pastors lament the unwillingness of congregants to accept church visitors whose socioeconomic status is obviously low. But God loves all kinds of people unconditionally and invites *anyone* to become a member of His family through faith in Jesus. And didn't Jesus walk among the poor and reach out to social outcasts: lepers, tax collectors, prostitutes, and drunkards? He received sinners as they were but did not leave them as they were. He changed their lives forever.

This study inspires us to relate to everyone as an object of God's love.

COMMENTARY

The context of this story is God's continuing faithfulness to Israel amid external dangers and internal faithlessness. Moses was dead, but God appointed Joshua to lead the people into the Promised Land. God said to Joshua, "As I was with Moses, so I will be with you; I will never leave you nor forsake you" (Josh. 1:5). Then God repeated two basic principles to guide Joshua. First, "Do not let this Book of the Law depart from your mouth; meditate on it day and night, so that you may be careful to do everything written in it" (1:8; see Deut. 4:1–14 for the similar command given to the people through Moses). Second, God repeated the injunction not to fear (Josh. 1:9; see Num. 21:34), for He was working ahead of Joshua to ensure the Israelites' victory. Of course, Israel would violate both of these principles.

Most striking is how the battles against the kings Sihon and Og were branded on the collective conscience of Israel. Because God worked specifically through Israelite history, the Old Testament preserves God's miraculous acts and recounts them as examples of God's faithfulness. We are used to reading recounts of the exodus, even in the New Testament. However, these two battles also played an important role, not only in this story, but in its larger context. In fact, these battles were used as historical markers for the giving of the Law in Deuteronomy 1:3–5. They were remembered in the time of Solomon. First Kings 4:19 describes Gilead as "the country of Sihon king of the Amorites and the country of Og king of Bashan." They were also referenced, along with the events in Joshua, when Ezra and Nehemiah reestablished the covenant (see Neh. 9:22–25).

Later we will examine how this came to be, but for now it is important to see the events in this story and in the whole book of Joshua not in isolation, but as a part of a greater whole, the history of the salvation of Israel.

Spying Out Jericho and the Whole Land (Josh. 2:1–7)

By sending spies, Joshua was following the military strategy of Moses. "After Moses had sent spies to Jazer, the Israelites captured its surrounding settlements and drove out the Amorites who were there" (Num. 21:32). Jericho was a fortified city just east of the Jordan River. It was considered the gateway to the west by the Israelites. Much intelligence could be gathered about the land of Canaan from such a city.

The NIV notes that the word translated **prostitute** in Joshua 2:1 could also be understood as "innkeeper." Either way, Rahab was on the edge of society. Interestingly, verse 15 tells us that her home was a part of the city wall. She was tolerated because her service was needed, but she was effectively a nonperson.

WORDS FROM WESLEY

Joshua 2:1

Two men—Not twelve, as Moses did, because those were to view the whole land, these but a small parcel of it. *To spy*—That is, to learn the state of the land and people. It is evident Joshua did not this out of distrust; it is probable, he had God's command and direction in it for the encouragement of himself and his army. *Secretly*—With reference not to his enemies, that being the practice of all spies, but to the Israelites; a good caution to prevent the inconveniency which possibly might have arisen, if their report had been discouraging. *Jericho*—That is, the land about Jericho, together with the city. The land and Jericho, that is, especially Jericho. *Harlot's*—So the Hebrew word is used, Judg. 11:1, and so it is rendered by two apostles, Heb. 11:31, James 2:25, such she either now was, or rather, had been formerly. (ENOT)

Note **the king of Jericho** (v. 2). During the times of this story, the land was dominated by city-states. That is, each city exerted the maximum independence it could depending upon its size and resources. While periodic dynasties arose that controlled groups of cities, the stronger cities usually reasserted their independence when the controlling king died or when the controlling city weakened or was captured. The fact that the king of Jericho received the report suggests that he, or the city itself, was considered a controlling factor in the area, and they were definitely asserting their independence.

Another characteristic of city-states in this time was that they generally had protective walls and gates. Thus, there is literary irony in the location of Rahab's home. It was the "crack" in the wall. There is also economic irony associated with the walls. Walled cities experienced population growth that often exhausted the food production within the walls. Therefore, the walled cities levied production taxes on unwalled villages and homes in exchange for protection. However, cities could outgrow the production taxes, which led to tax increases, which eventually led to revolts. Thus, the irony was that the wall built to protect the city from the outside actually weakened the city from the inside.

The gates were closed at or near sunset and not generally reopened until dawn. That is why Rahab's story was convincing to the pursuers. If the spies wanted to see other parts of the land, or if they were wary of being trapped in Jericho for the night, they would have left before the city gate was closed. There was no other way out. So the spies were safe until morning since the gate was closed after the pursuers left (v. 7).

This part of the story reminds us of the Hebrew midwives who lied to the Egyptians in order to save the Hebrew babies. It also reminds us of Christians who lied to Gestapo soldiers in order to save Jews. These are interesting examples of the descriptive nature of the Bible. All of these people acted within the will of God but used deception to do so.

WORDS FROM WESLEY

Joshua 2:4

And the woman—Or, *But the woman had taken*—*and had hid them*, before the messengers came from the king; as soon as the understood from her neighbours, that there was a suspicion of the matter, and guessed that search would be made. And this is justly mentioned as a great and generous act of faith, Heb. 11:31, for the apparently ventured her life upon a steadfast persuasion of the truth of God's word and promise given to the Israelites. *Whence they were*—Her answer contained in these and the following words, was false, and therefore unquestionably sinful; tho' her intention was good therein. But it is very probable, she being an heathen, might think, that an officious lie is not unlawful. (ENOT)

The Story Goes Ahead of the Spies (Josh. 2:8–11)

The stories of the defeat of Sihon and Og are recounted in Numbers 21:21–35 and Deuteronomy 2:24—3:11. That these battles were seared on the collective Israelite memory and the memory of their neighbors is evidenced in Joshua 2:10. Similar statements are recorded from the Gibeonites in Joshua 9:9–10: "Your servants have come from a very distant country because of the fame of the LORD your God. For we have heard reports of him: all that he did in Egypt, and all that he did to the two kings of the Amorites east of the Jordan—Sihon king of Heshbon, and Og king of Bashan, who reigned in Ashtaroth."

The question is how these people heard these stories. One possible answer is through Psalms 135 and 136. Compare Joshua 2:8–11 with Psalm 135:5–12. Also note the comparison with Psalm 136:10–22.

If these songs were sung faithfully by the Israelites, it is possible that they were the media through which the stories were spread. Battle songs would be interesting to other people who came in contact with the Israelites, especially ones that recounted the defeat of strong kings. In an age of limited literacy, songs would serve as an effective way to spread stories. Psalm 136 seems more developed than Psalm 135 and is probably dependent upon it for the material. This is further evidence of the lasting effect the defeat of Sihon and Og had on the Israelite community. These events were evidently used as propaganda with positive results against future enemies.

Not only were stories of the battles preserved, they were issued as evidence that the Lord had already given the land to the Israelites "as an inheritance." That is, the Israelites had the right to the land regardless of who was already there. It was not because they claimed it, but because their God—the living God who had created everything and thus had the right to give as He saw fit—had given them the land. Interestingly, ancient documents show that all the civilizations in this area were concerned with property rights within their legal systems. The "inheritance" language would have been quite powerful in their understanding. If human inheritance was guarded by the law, then divine inheritance was unquestionable. Thus, the hearts of those in Jericho failed because of the Israelites. If their God had given them the powerful kings Sihon and Og and delivered them from Egypt, then surely Jericho was theirs to take. Everyone had heard the songs.

WORDS FROM WESLEY

Joshua 2:12

By the Lord—By your God who is the only true God: so she owns His worship, one eminent act whereof is swearing by His name. *My father's house*—My near kindred, which she particularly names, ver. 13, husband and children it seems she had none. And for herself, it was needless to speak, it being a plain and undeniable duty to save their preserver. *True token*—Either an assurance that you will preserve me and mine from the common ruin: or a token which I may produce as a witness of this agreement, and a means of my security. This is all that she asks. But God did for her more than she could ask or think. She was afterwards advanced to be a princess in Israel, the wife of Salmon and one of the ancestors of Christ. (ENOT)

The Covenant (Josh. 2:12–14, 17–21)

Rahab wanted assurances that her actions on behalf of the spies would result not only in her salvation, but also in the salvation of her entire family. So she made a pact with them. There are two parallels to this story. Most evident is the parallel between the blood of the lambs placed on the doorposts in the exodus story and the scarlet cord placed in the window. The second parallel is between the covenant between God and Abraham in Genesis 15 and Joshua 2:19–20. In Genesis, God passed between the severed offering animals to accept Abraham's blood on His hands if He was not faithful to the covenant. In the same way, the spies,

God's representatives, accepted the same toward Rahab. Granted, this is more of an echo than a parallel, but the agreement here was as much between Rahab and the Lord as it was between Rahab and the spies.

Therefore, it illustrates the motif of the "two ways"—the way of obedience that leads to life and the way of disobedience that leads to death. This is one of the themes of the entire Old Testament. It transcends nationalities, gender, and social status. This is the way the national God of the Israelites claimed authority over the world. Whoever was obedient to Him was included in His covenant of life. We see in Matthew 1:5 that Rahab gave birth to Boaz, as also recorded in the book of Ruth. Thus the prostitute was included in the lineage of Jesus, God's Savior of the entire world. So the covenant was complete. Her entire family was brought in.

WORDS FROM WESLEY

Joshua 2:19

Upon his head—The blame of his death shall rest wholly upon himself, as being occasioned by his own neglect of the means of safety. *Our head*—We are willing to bear the sin, and shame, and punishment of it. (ENOT)

DISCUSSION

Espionage, intrigue, suspense, and surprise—all these elements run through the story of scouting out Jericho's defenses.

1. What do you think Joshua wanted to accomplish by sending two spies to Jericho?

2. Read Joshua 2:1–15. Why do you agree or disagree that God directed the spies to Rahab's house? If you agree, what might have been His reasons for leading them there?

3. What indication do you find in verses 8–11 that Israel could have destroyed Jericho at an earlier time?

4. Why do you agree that most of our fears are unfounded?

5. Do you believe it is ethical to use deception to save lives, for example, in time of war?

6. What do you find commendable about Rahab?

7. Do you think the scarlet cord (vv. 18, 21) symbolizes the blood of Christ that saves believing sinners from destruction? Why or why not?

8. Read Matthew 1:5. What divine characteristics do you see in the fact that Rahab became an ancestor of Jesus Christ?

PRAYER

Father, thank You for the "scarlet cord" of Your salvation, pointing ultimately to Your Son. Forgive us for judging others by their past or their background. And grant us wisdom to find Your provision in unexpected places.

WE WORSHIP AND GOD WORKS

Joshua 3:5–17; 4:4–7

Consecrate yourselves, watch what God is doing, and remember.

Our impossible circumstances are God's magnificent opportunities. When we face a medical crisis, He gets us through it. When our finances shrink, He stretches our resources and meets our needs. When we are unemployed, He rallies friends and loved ones to help. When we think we can't go on, His everlasting arms uphold us. When we think disappointments will crush us, He shows us they are His appointments to grow us.

This study shows how God made a way across the Jordan for His people when the river was at flood stage, not when it was ankle deep. By faith the people stepped into the raging river. This study inspires us to trust God and "get our feet wet" when life seems impossible.

COMMENTARY

Israel had waited a long time for this day. Some six hundred years ago God had covenanted with Abraham to give them the land of Canaan. They always knew it would be theirs, but the fertile, strategic strip of land seemed always to be just beyond their reach. And now they stood at the doorway to Canaan. But one obstacle remained: the flooded Jordan River. Though normally an easily passable stream, at flood stage the Jordan was formidable. Its waters were swift and treacherous. Once again the Israelites were at the end of their resources. Once again they needed to experience the intervention of the God who had led them there.

And God did not disappoint them.

Consecration: Preparation for the Miracle (Josh. 3:5)

Joshua addressed the people of Israel: **"Consecrate your-selves, for tomorrow the LORD will do amazing things among you"** (v. 5). The Hebrew here for **amazing things** means something out of the ordinary, a miracle. God was going to step into history again to accomplish the impossible. In order for the people to be ready for the miracle, they had to prepare. Not just outwardly or militarily—they had to prepare their hearts.

The call to consecration involved washing their clothes (see Ex. 19:10–14), an outward expression of their inward cleansing. It was a call to solemnity, to serious consideration of what lay ahead. It was a call to repentance and complete devotion to God in anticipation of what He was going to do.

Cooperation: Participation in the Miracle (Josh. 3:6–17)

Normally it was the Kohathites who were charged with carrying the ark of the covenant and the other sacred furnishings of the Tent of Meeting in the Israelites' travels (see Num. 4:15). But this was no normal occasion. It was a religious procession, and so it was fitting that the **priests** (Josh. 3:6) would take the uncovered ark and lead the way with it. The **ark of the covenant** was a visible symbol of God's presence. And now the ark, which was usually in the midst of the camp, was to **pass on ahead of the people** (v. 6), symbolizing to all Israel that God himself was leading the way.

WORDS FROM WESLEY

Joshua 3:6

Before the people—Not in the middle of them, as you used to do. (ENOT)

But they would have to follow. In the desert, the Lord had led them by a cloud by day and a pillar of fire by night (Ex. 33:9–10; Num. 14:14). Now this was gone. They had to walk by faith if they wanted to see the miracle.

And the LORD said to Joshua, "Today I will begin to exalt you in the eyes of all Israel, so they may know that I am with you as I was with Moses" (Josh. 3:7). The miracle about to take place had more than one purpose. It would be necessary for entering the land, but it would also be a testimony that God had ordained Joshua as Israel's leader. After the miraculous crossing of the Red Sea forty years earlier, Exodus 14:31 tells us, "And when the Israelites saw the great power the LORD displayed against the Egyptians, the people feared the LORD and put their trust in him and in Moses his servant." And the present miracle would have a similar effect: "That day the LORD exalted Joshua in the sight of all Israel; and they revered him all the days of his life, just as they had revered Moses" (Josh. 4:14).

The miracle would also serve as a visible reminder of God's active presence among them and as a guarantee that He would fulfill His promises. **This is how you will know that the living God is among you and that he will certainly drive out before you the Canaanites** (3:10). In the Hebrew text there is no article ("the") before **living God**; the emphasis is on **living**. The miracle would show God as vastly superior to the gods of wood and stone worshiped by the peoples they were about to conquer. The God of Israel was One who could see and hear, who was personal and involved in their lives. He was a God of power, in control over the elements He created and the nations of the earth, vastly superior to any so-called god worshiped in Canaan. As the living God, He had the right to determine who would occupy His land. He would drive out all the inhabitants of Canaan: the **Canaanites**, who inhabited the lowlands of the seacoast and the Jordan valley, the **Hittites** to the south, the **Hivites** in the northern region of

Mount Hermon, the **Perizzites** in the central highlands, the **Girgashites** near the Sea of Galilee, the **Amorites** who inhabited the mountainous regions, and the **Jebusites** occupying the region around Jerusalem (v. 10). God was greater than all these nations. He was—and is—the **Lord of all the earth** (vv. 11, 13).

WORDS FROM WESLEY

Joshua 3:10

Ye shall know—By experience and sensible evidence. *The living God*—Not a dull, dead, senseless God, such as the gods of the nations are; but a God of life, and power, and activity to watch over you, and work for you. *Among you*—Is present with you to strengthen and help you. (ENOT)

Joshua foretold what was about to happen: **And as soon as the priests . . . set foot in the Jordan, its waters flowing downstream will be cut off and stand up in a heap** (v. 13). God was about to perform a miracle curiously similar to the crossing of the Red Sea (see Ex. 14:21–22 and Ps. 114, where the two events are linked). It was a new generation that needed a new miracle. But this time, much more faith was required. In the crossing of the Red Sea, a strong wind blew all night long, parting the waters and drying the ground before the Israelites stepped in to cross; this time the priests would have to take a step of faith and set foot in the river before the miracle happened. If they wanted to participate in the miracle, they would have to cooperate with God's plan. They would have to do it His way, walking in faith.

The crossing of the Jordan took place in the month of Nissan (the first month, March–April; see Josh. 4:19) at the time of the barley harvest when the spring rains and the melted snow from Mount Hermon swelled the Jordan River. **Now the Jordan is at flood stage all during harvest** (3:15). The Hebrew says the Jordan was "flowing over all its banks." There was a torrent of water. It was an intimidating sight, but the priests took God at His word and stepped into the water. And **as soon as . . . their feet touched the water's edge, the water from upstream stopped flowing. It piled up in a heap a great distance away, at a town called Adam** (vv. 15–16). The miracle was immediate. And it was just as God had promised through Joshua.

WORDS FROM WESLEY
Joshua 3:13

The ark of the Lord—That so it may appear this is the Lord's doing, and that in pursuance of His covenant made with Israel. *Of all the earth*—The Lord of all this globe of earth and water, who therefore can dispose of this river and the adjoining land as He pleaseth. (ENOT)

We don't know exactly where this miracle took place, but verse 16 tells us that **the people crossed over opposite Jericho**. Two million people had to cross. And they had to stay a thousand yards away from the ark (v. 4). It is probable that the Israelites were spread out over miles as they crossed the Jordan.

The water piled up **at a town called Adam** (v. 16), generally associated with Tell ed-Damiyeh, sixteen miles north of the ford opposite Jericho. On December 8, 1267, the high banks of the Jordan near this tell collapsed, damming the river for ten hours. On July 11, 1927, the same thing occurred, this time damming the Jordan for twenty-one hours. The Jordan River, geologists tell us, follows a fault line, making the region prone to small earthquakes (which may be referenced in Ps. 114:4, 6–7). If God used a natural phenomenon, such as an earthquake, to induce this miracle, it was a miracle nonetheless. His timing was perfect. And the **priests . . . stood firm on dry ground in the middle of the**

Jordan, while all Israel passed by until the whole nation had completed the crossing on dry ground (Josh. 3:17). Without an all-night wind (as in the Red Sea parting), the ground was made instantly dry and firm. **Dry ground**—*harabah* in Hebrew—means "not covered with water," not necessarily powder dry. But it was dry enough to make passage safe and effortless.

Crossing the Jordan into Canaan marked a new beginning for Israel. They were leaving their past behind. They were entering into a hostile land. It had been promised to them, but they would have to fight for it. It wouldn't be easy, but if they continued to follow the Lord and obey Him, they would be part of the miracle of the acquisition of the land.

Commemoration: Preservation of the Miracle (Josh. 4:4–7)

Before the Israelites had crossed the Jordan, Joshua set apart twelve men, one from each of the tribes of Israel, for a special task (4:4; see 3:12). Now he commanded them, **"Go over before the ark** [not before in time, but "in the presence of" the ark] **... into the middle of the Jordan. Each of you is to take up a stone on his shoulder"** (4:5). These men took their stones from the very spot where the priests had stood with the ark of the covenant (v. 2), and they set them up (either in a pile or a circle) at Gilgal, where the Israelites set up camp (v. 20). The rough memorial was **to serve as a sign among** them (v. 6). It was to be a visual reminder of the miracle that had taken place. In 1 Samuel 11:15 and 2 Samuel 19:15, national gatherings were later held here, probably because of this faith-evoking memorial. It was a reminder to them, but it was also to be a testimony to future generations. **"In the future, when your children ask you, 'What do these stones mean?' tell them ... these stones are to be a memorial to the people of Israel forever"** (Josh. 4:6–7).

God was always concerned that faith in Him be passed down from one generation to another (see Ps. 145:4). The sacrifices and feasts, the Sabbath celebration, the rituals and traditions—all these were tools for teaching successive generations about the God of Israel (see Deut. 4:9; 6:6–9). They would be reminders of His miracles and His expectations. They would serve as an enduring testimony. The history of God's work among them would be preserved and recounted, invoking faith in each new generation.

WORDS FROM WESLEY

Joshua 4:6

A sign—A monument or memorial of this day's work. (ENOT)

Today we rarely use symbols as reminders of God's faithfulness. But we have the written Word of God, the testimony not only of the Israelites, but also of the apostles who bore witness to the greatest miracle of all—the resurrection of Jesus Christ. And we have our own miracle stories of God's work in our individual lives. We have an obligation to preserve these miracles, to find a way to commemorate them, and to celebrate them so our children, and our children's children, hear about the greatness of the living God.

DISCUSSION

Moving is an adventure, especially when it involves entering an area where the locals will oppose you with all their might.

1. According to Joshua 3:2–4, what instructions concerning the ark were the Israelites supposed to follow?

2. Why do you think the people were commanded to keep a distance of about a thousand yards between them and the ark?

3. Why is it so important to be consecrated to the Lord before engaging the enemy?

4. Compare verses 7 and 15. Why did it require an act of faith to obey Joshua's instructions?

5. When did you recently meet a challenge by stepping out in faith?

6. What leadership qualities do you admire in Joshua? In the priests?

7. What was the intended purpose of the monument of stones (vv. 4–7)?

8. What are some excellent ways to remind future generations of the Lord's wonderful deeds?

PRAYER

Lord, You are so good to us. Thank You for parting the "Jordan Rivers" in our lives. Help us to recognize Your gracious hand and to remember Your work on our behalf.

4

SIN INFECTS AND AFFECTS

Joshua 7:2–13, 19–26

Sin is infectious, and its effects are extensive.

Toys were almost a fatal attraction for a three-year-old boy in Sydney, Australia. Lured by the toys he saw in a vending machine at an Australian shopping center and separated from his mother, little Callum must have climbed into the machine through the delivery chute. He reached the toys, but couldn't climb back out. When his mother called his name, he answered from inside the machine. Fortunately rescuers were able to remove the door from the back of the machine and extricate the boy. He had been trapped for about an hour.

This study emphasizes the harm covetousness can cause, and it motivates us to make God's will our highest priority.

COMMENTARY

Joshua 7 deals with the Israelites' initial attempts to capture the city of Ai. Ai is located in the hill country about fifteen miles west of Jericho. Joshua 7:2–13, 19–26 is part of the larger literary unit of 7:1 — 8:29 that has the seven subsections.

Initial Attack and the Subsequent Defeat (Josh. 7:2–5)

Totally unaware that a sin had been committed, Joshua sent out spies to investigate the situation of Ai: **Now Joshua sent men from Jericho to Ai . . . and told them, "Go up and spy out the region." So the men went up and spied out Ai** (v. 2). Earlier, when the spies were sent to check out Jericho, God gave a promise: "I have delivered Jericho into your hands" (6:2) and specific instructions about the battle strategy (6:3–5). Joshua moved against Jericho in complete obedience to the divine instructions. Here in chapter 7, there is no divine assurance of victory or battle plan for Ai. In the absence of such, one would expect Joshua to make an inquiry of God so as to secure them (see Num. 27:20–21). An inquiry of God likely would have revealed to Joshua the divine disfavor (compare 1 Sam. 14:36–43). But Joshua forged ahead without any divine directive, following instead the suggestion of the spies: **Send two or three thousand men to take it. . . . So about three thousand men went up** (Josh. 7:3–4).

Unlike the Jericho narrative, which ended with the people's triumphant victory due to God's fighting the battle for them, the Ai account tersely notes: **but they were routed by the men of Ai, who killed about thirty-six of them. They chased the Israelites from the city gate as far as the stone quarries and struck them down on the slopes** (vv. 4–5). Thirty-six might seem like an insignificant number of losses, but given the lack of casualties against the more daunting city of Jericho, the loss of thirty-six probably seemed excessive.

Besides the military defeat of the Israelites, this was also a psychological defeat, as **the hearts of the people melted and became like water** (v. 5). Whereas before, at Jericho, the Canaanites' hearts were melting in fear before the Israelites (2:11, 24; 5:1), now the situation was completely reversed.

Joshua's Prayer (Josh. 7:6–9)

In response to the defeat, Joshua and the elders of Israel went through typical gestures of mourning: he **tore his clothes**; he **fell facedown to the ground**, and **the elders** did likewise and also **sprinkled dust on their heads** (v. 6). These acts indicated a person's humility in the midst of sadness and contrition. Joshua did these in the presence **of the LORD**, that is, **before the ark** (v. 6).

WORDS FROM WESLEY

Joshua 7:6

Rent his clothes—In testimony of great sorrow, for the loss felt, the consequent mischief feared, and the sin which he suspected. *His face*—In deep humiliation and fervent supplication. *Until the eventide*—Continuing the whole day in fasting and prayer. *Put dust upon their heads*—As was usual in case of grief and astonishment. (ENOT)

In his prayer, Joshua questioned what the Lord was doing, spoke about the tragedy of the event, and speculated about the future ramifications of it (vv. 7–9). Only in verse 9 is there an indirect petition in the form of a question, requesting some kind of divine intervention (**What then will you do . . . ?**). Joshua perceived the defeat as an indication of the Lord's disfavor, but he did not understand the cause. He seemed to view the divine disfavor as a result of a fickleness or capriciousness on the part of God. In verse 7, he attributed negative intents and motives to God (**Why did you ever bring this people across the Jordan to deliver us into the hands of the Amorites to destroy us?**) and desired that the previous condition could prevail (**If only we had been content to stay on the other side of the Jordan!**).

In verses 8–9, Joshua raised two legitimate issues. The first was that, in light of the Israelites being routed, **the Canaanites** might now have the courage to counterattack (v. 9). God had expressed His intent that the other nations would "fear him," and such had been the nations' response (see 2:9–11, 24; 5:1). But now that psychological and spiritual advantage was in jeopardy, with potentially dire ramifications for the Israelites.

The second issue was the Lord's perceived reputation. If the Israelites were exterminated by God or their enemies, or merely allowed to be shamefully defeated in battle, such would result in derision and contempt for the Israelites' God.

Divine Response (Josh. 7:10–13)

The divine response to Joshua's prayer subdivides into two sections: verses 10–12, the divine indictment for the sin; and verses 13–15, the instructions for restoration. Whereas Joshua's prayer focused on God's role in the situation, the Lord focused completely on the Israelites' role.

God's response indicated that Joshua's prayer was not wholly appropriate: **"What are you doing down on your face?"** (v. 10). In light of the divine promise of success and defeat of the enemies (1:2–6), Joshua's question (7:7) suggesting that God intended to deliver the Israelites to their enemies was an invalid accusation. And in light of the divine command to cross the Jordan (1:2), Joshua's declaration (7:7) that they should not have done so was an inappropriate regret of doing what God commanded. Finally, since success was to be contingent upon the people's obedience (1:7–9), Joshua needed not to be in a posture of questioning; the lack of success indicated disobedience.

WORDS FROM WESLEY

Joshua 7:10

What profits prayer itself, unless
We put the cursed thing away?
Lord, let us first the sin redress,
And then against the judgment pray. (PW, vol. 9, 122)

God stressed that the defeat was not His fault, but rather Israel's. In 7:11, the indictment moved from a general expression (**Israel has sinned; they have violated my covenant**) to a delineation of the specific sins committed (**They have taken some of the**

devoted things; they have stolen, they have lied, they have put them with their own possessions). Although only Achan had committed the specific action, the whole nation was held culpable.

In verse 12, the consequences were expressed first with reference to the specifics of the occasion: **That is why the Israelites cannot stand against their enemies; they turn their backs and run because they have been made liable to destruction.** Then a more generalized ramification was noted: **I will not be with you anymore** (v. 12). The latter, as it reflected a future possibility, made it clear that the consequences were more serious than this one defeat. But at this point, the removal of the divine presence was only a hypothetical possibility. It would only occur if the people did not deal with the sin (v. 12). The opportunity for restoration was offered to the people, and God then detailed the means by which such could take place (vv. 13–15).

The initial instruction in verse 13 was for the people to prepare themselves: **"Go, consecrate the people. Tell them, 'Consecrate yourselves in preparation.'"** The phrase is literally "make holy" in the sense of purifying so as to come into the presence of the Lord. The sacredness of the holy assembly that would occur the next day was emphasized through the necessity of the people's ritual purifying in preparation for it.

WORDS FROM WESLEY

Joshua 7:13

It is a marvellous thing that Achan did not on this occasion acknowledge his crime; but this is to be imputed to the heart-hardening power of sin, which makes men, grow worse and worse; to his pride, being loath to take to himself the shame of such a mischievous and infamous action; and to his vain conceit, whereby he might think others were guilty as well as he, and some of them might be taken, and he escape. (ENOT)

Israel's Discernment and Punishment of the Sin (Josh. 7:19–26)

Whereas disobedience had disrupted the covenant relationship with God, the people were particularly careful to be fully observant of what God told them to do, so as to assure restoration.

The Public Confession (Josh. 7:19–21). Although Achan was the one "chosen," the verification occurred first through a public admission of guilt. Achan's confession involved three things: an acknowledgment of sin (v. 20), a description of the specific thing he did (vv. 20–21), and information about where the loot was hidden (v. 21). The fact that Achan concealed the items indicates that he sought to keep his action a secret. His disclosure of where the items were was important because the Lord had commanded that for restoration to take place the people needed to "destroy whatever among you is devoted to destruction" (7:12).

WORDS FROM WESLEY

Joshua 7:19

My son—So he calls him, to shew, that this severe inquisition and sentence did not proceed from any hatred to his person, which he loved as a father doth his son, and as a prince ought to do each of his subjects. *The Lord God of Israel*—As thou hast highly dishonoured Him, now take the blame to thyself, and ascribe unto God the glory of His omniscience in knowing thy sin, of His justice in punishing it in thee, and others for thy sake; of His omnipotency, which was obstructed by thee; and of His kindness and faithfulness to His people, which was eclipsed by thy wickedness; all which will now be evident by thy sin confessed and punished. (ENOT)

Verification through Producing the Evidence (Josh. 7:22–23). The messengers dispatched by Joshua found the items, just as Achan had said (vv. 21–22). The stolen goods were then **brought . . . to Joshua and all the Israelites and** were **spread . . . out before the Lord** (v. 23). The "devoted things," which belonged to the Lord, were returned to their rightful owner.

Punishment of Achan (Josh. 7:24–26). **Joshua** then **took Achan** along with the stolen devoted items—**the silver, the robe, the gold wedge**—and all that belonged to him to the place where they would be executed. The place was called **the Valley of Achor** (v. 24), "the Valley of Trouble." It was so named because of the play on the term in Joshua's statement in verse 25, which echoed the command in 6:18, where it is declared that if they kept any of the devoted things they would "bring trouble on" ("bring disaster on") Israel.

The punishment is described in 7:25. First Achan was **stoned**, then the other living beings (family and animals) were stoned, and then everything was **burned** (v. 25), after which the ash remains were buried by covering them with **a large pile of rocks** (v. 26).

On the surface, the punishment seems harsh. After all, Achan confessed and "came clean" with respect to what he had done. Yet no mercy was extended in the sense of him being granted forgiveness and his life spared. Achan's punishment must be seen in light of two things. First, the people had made a pledge: "Whoever rebels against your word and does not obey your words . . . will be put to death" (1:18). Thus Achan's punishment adhered to that pledge. Second, the Lord had specifically commanded in this case, "He who is caught with the devoted things shall be destroyed by fire" (7:15).

Another issue related to the severity of the punishment is that Achan's family was killed and all his belongings destroyed. Nothing in the text implicates his family (his sons and daughters) as coconspirators or even them being aware of his actions. Any theory of his family's collaboration still does not explain the inclusion of his **cattle, donkeys and sheep** (v. 24). The inclusiveness of the punishment revolves around the nature of the stolen items. Since Ai and all its inhabitants and contents were "liable to destruction," when Achan took some of those devoted things, he aligned himself with Ai and also became "liable to destruction" (v. 12), coming under the command in 6:17–18.

Two "memorials" of this event served as reminders (that is, warnings) to future generations about the consequences of disobedience. One was the visible burial pile of rocks, which remained **to this day** (7:26; that is, the author's day). The other was the name of the place, the **Valley of Achor** ("Trouble"), by which it had been called **ever since** (v. 26). Those "memorials" provided the catalyst for the continued recapitulation of the story and its spiritual lessons, just like the "memorial" stones set up at the crossing of the Jordan, which were there "to this day" (3:8–9, 20–24).

Once the guilty party had been punished, **then the LORD turned from his fierce anger** (7:26). The restoration process was complete. The rest of the story is in Joshua 8. Once the rectification of the disobedience had been achieved, victory over Ai occurred as the people trusted in God's promises and followed His battle plan. Defeat due to disobedience (ch. 7) gave way to victory because of obedience (ch. 8).

DISCUSSION

One drop of ink in a glass of water taints the whole glass. Discuss if one sin can hurt an entire family—or an entire nation.

1. We do not read that Joshua and the Israelites consulted the Lord before they attacked Ai. Why didn't they do so?

2. Joshua consulted the Lord after Israel's defeat. Have you prayed after a defeat that probably would not have occurred if you had prayed before the incident? What was the occasion?

3. Why did Israel suffer defeat at the hands of the men of Ai (Josh. 7:10–12)?

4. What would it take to regain the Lord's favor and help (vv. 12–13)?

5. Why do you agree or disagree that church discipline is almost archaic?

6. What excuses might a church use for failing to exercise church discipline?

7. What sin led to Achan's deceptive act? Why do you agree or disagree that the sin you identified is prevalent among Christians today?

8. Achan and his family were punished by death. How would you respond to the claim that we should love and forgive every offender, because none of us is perfect?

PRAYER

Father, search our hearts and reveal all our sins, great and small, because they're all evil in Your sight. Keep us from the slightest deviation from Your will. Please forgive us.

5

THE SECRETS OF WHOLEHEARTED DEVOTION

Joshua 14:5–15

Wholehearted devotion to God is the key to finishing well.

It's called a bucket list—a list of things a person wants to do before he or she "kicks the bucket." A bucket list may include such feats as climbing Mount Everest, parachuting from an airplane, traveling around the world, skiing in Aspen, or peering into a live volcano. However, it's highly unlikely that a bucket list would include the feat of routing a well-armed enemy from a mountain. But that is precisely what eighty-five-year-old Caleb did by faith.

This study will motivate you to wholly follow the Lord and rely on Him all the days of your life.

COMMENTARY

Some forty-five years before the time of this study, Joshua and Caleb had gone on a mission along with ten other Israelites. Their task was to explore the land of Canaan that God had promised to Israel. The exploration was preliminary preparation for the people of Israel to possess the Promised Land. The twelve spies set out from Kadesh Barnea, consisting of one representative from each of the tribes of Israel. For forty days they explored the length and breadth of the land God had promised to give them.

Upon their return to Kadesh Barnea, they presented amazing spoils from the Promised Land. Evidently, all twelve of the spies gave glowing reports about the land and its bounty. However, their reports were not all positive. Only Joshua and Caleb reported that the Israelites should press ahead, trusting God to give them success in their conquest. The other ten men were fearful, and those ten predicted defeat for Israel. They reported that the land was populated with many giants and that the people of the land were far too powerful for the Israelites to succeed. They were sure that if Israel entered the land they would be defeated. However, Joshua and Caleb were confident that God would provide the power to conquer the land and its people. They urged the Israelites to press forward and enter the land immediately. Unfortunately, the majority opinion swayed the multitude, and the Israelites rebelled against the Lord by refusing to enter the land of promise there at Kadesh Barnea.

Their disobedience was followed by tragedy. God's anger raged against the people, and He promised that, because of their disobedience, every adult among the multitude of Israelites would die in the wilderness. There were only two exceptions—Joshua and Caleb. Because of their faithfulness, God promised that Joshua and Caleb would be rewarded. Not only would they survive to enter the Promised Land, they would also be given possessions in the land. In this study, Caleb was ready to claim that possession that had been promised to him so many years earlier.

Caleb Approached Joshua about His Inheritance (Josh. 14:5–6)

As the Israelites gathered at Gilgal, most of the land was conquered. It was time to divide the land between the tribes and then to further divide the land between the individual families of each tribe (14:1–5). Now, even though there were pockets of resistance remaining, it was time to settle in the land. East of the Jordan, the land had already been assigned to Reuben, Gad, and half of the tribe of Manasseh (13:8–31). Now, **the men of Judah approached Joshua at Gilgal** to receive their allotment (14:6). Caleb was one of the prominent members of the tribe of Judah; he was the oldest surviving member. He came to Joshua and reminded him of God's special promise made to them: **You**

know what the LORD said to Moses the man of God at Kadesh Barnea about you and me (v. 6).

WORDS FROM WESLEY

Joshua 14:8

I wholly followed the Lord—Which self-commendation is justifiable, because it was necessary, as being the ground of his petition. Therefore it was not vain glory in him to speak it: no more than it is for those, who have God's spirit witnessing with their spirits, that they are the children of God, humbly and thankfully to tell others, for their encouragement, what God hath done for their souls. (ENOT)

Caleb Reminded Joshua of His Faithfulness (Josh. 14:7–9)

Caleb reminded Joshua that the promise had been made back when Caleb was only **forty years old** (v. 7), and now he was eighty-five years old (v. 10). Forty-five years earlier, Caleb had trusted God and His power, giving a report that he believed Israel was able to conquer the land. **"But my brothers who went up with me made the hearts of the people melt with fear. I, however, followed the LORD my God wholeheartedly"** (v. 8). For this faithfulness, God had promised Caleb **the land on which his feet had walked** (v. 9). Other than in this passage, Hebron was not specified in Scripture as the land promised to Caleb, but here Caleb and Joshua seem to understand that the promise was related to that specific area of the hill country of Judah (v. 12). Caleb continued his request, **"So on that day Moses swore to me, 'The land on which your feet have walked will be your inheritance and that of your children forever, because you have followed the LORD my God wholeheartedly'"** (v. 9). God had blessed Caleb and Joshua with long life, and now they were the only two adults who had survived the wilderness wanderings to enter the land of promise.

WORDS FROM WESLEY

Joshua 14:10

Forty-five years—Whereof thirty-eight years were spent in the wilderness, and seven since they came into Canaan. The longer we live the more sensible we should be, of God's goodness to us in keeping us alive! Of His care in prolonging our frail lives, His patience in prolonging our forfeited lives! And shall not the life thus kept by His providence, be devoted to His praise? (ENOT)

Years before, at Kadesh Barnea, Caleb and Joshua had shown great courage as they urged the people to move forward and not to rebel against God. In fact, because they went against majority opinion, "the whole assembly talked about stoning them" (Num. 14:10). When the people rebelled, Moses and Aaron fell on their faces and interceded for them. Because of their intercession, God forgave the Israelites, and He would not destroy them completely. Still God pronounced: "Not one of them will ever see the land I promised on oath to their forefathers. No one who has treated me with contempt will ever see it. But because my servant Caleb has a different spirit and follows me wholeheartedly, I will bring him into the land he went to, and his descendants will inherit it" (Num. 14:23–24). The passage goes on to contrast the consequence of the unfaithfulness of the others with the promise to Joshua and Caleb. The ten men "responsible for spreading the bad report about the land were struck down and died of a plague before the LORD. Of the men who went to explore the land, only Joshua son of Nun and Caleb son of Jephunneh survived" (Num. 14:37–38). Caleb's steadfastness was rewarded.

God's Faithfulness to Caleb (Josh. 14:10–11)

For forty years, **Israel moved about in the desert** (v. 10). They finally entered the land, but only after passing through many perils. And those who had rebelled at Kadesh Barnea, had died, one by one, along the way. Now only Joshua and Caleb were left. Not only had Caleb survived to the age of eighty-five, he had survived in splendid health. He told Joshua, **"I am still as strong today as the day Moses sent me out; I'm just as vigorous to go out to battle now as I was then"** (v. 11). God had so blessed Caleb that his statement appears miraculous to us today as it must have appeared there at Gilgal. His vigor at age eighty-five was still as great as it had been at age forty. But Caleb wasn't through yet; now he was ready for his next challenge.

Caleb Claimed His Land (Josh. 14:12)

Caleb claimed that Hebron and the area surrounding that city were promised to him. The city of Hebron was in the hill country of Judah, and was the first city visited by the twelve spies (Num. 13:32). The area was occupied by the Anakites, giants according to the report of the ten spies (Num. 13:33). In that report, the Hebrews "seemed like grasshoppers" beside these giants. Furthermore, **their cities were large and fortified** (Josh. 14:12). Caleb was confident that he would have success: **"The LORD helping me, I will drive them out just as he said"** (v. 12). Giants and fortified cities did not trouble Caleb, for he trusted that God's power would give him what he had been promised those many years earlier. At eighty-five, with the vigor of a forty-year-old, he was ready to tackle the task.

WORDS FROM WESLEY

Joshua 14:12

This mountain—That is, this mountainous country. He names the country rather than the cities, because the cities were given to the Levites, chap. 21:11, 13. *Thou heardest*—Didst understand, both by the reports of others, and by thy own observation. Hearing, the sense by which we get knowledge, is often put for knowing or understanding. *If the Lord will be with me*—A modest and pious expression, signifying both the absolute necessity of God's help, and his godly fear, left God for his sins should deny His assistance to him; for although he was well assured in general, that God would crown His people with success in this war, yet he might doubt of his particular success in this or that enterprise. *To drive them out*—Out of their fastnesses where they yet remain, Caleb desires this difficult work as a testimony of his own faith, and as a motive to quicken his brethren to the like attempts. (ENOT)

We learn a bit more about Caleb's conquest of Hebron in Joshua 15:13–19. "Caleb drove out the three Anakites—Sheshai, Ahiman and Talmai—descendants of Anak" (15:14). Then Caleb promised his daughter Achsah in marriage to the man who would conquer Debir (also named Kiriath Sepher). His relative Othniel, possibly a cousin or nephew, accepted the challenge and took the city. Thus Othniel was given Achsah in marriage, and Othniel became Caleb's son-in-law. At Achsah's request, Caleb also gave them "upper and lower springs" (15:19). In that desert region water was a scarce resource, so this was a very valuable gift.

Joshua Granted Caleb His Inheritance (Josh. 14:13–15)

Clearly Joshua also understood that Hebron had been promised to Caleb. As an older comrade and as leader of the people, **Joshua blessed Caleb son of Jephunneh and gave him Hebron as his inheritance** (v. 13). The text then brought the record up-to-date as of the time of its writing: **Hebron has belonged to**

Caleb son of Jephunneh the Kenizzite ever since, because he followed the LORD, the God of Israel, wholeheartedly (v. 14).

Also, a historical note is given, telling us that **Hebron** was earlier called **Kiriath Arba** (town of Arba) **after Arba, who was the greatest man among the Anakites** (v. 15).

WORDS FROM WESLEY

Joshua 14:15

A great man—In stature, and strength, and dignity, and authority, as being the progenitor of Anak, the father of those famous giants called Anakims. (ENOT)

In a further note the text tells us, **then the land had rest from war** (v. 15). The general war of the conquest was over. Future wars were to be more localized as the Israelites continued to root out some of the remaining Canaanites. Unfortunately, not all the enemy was conquered, and the nations remaining continually caused trouble for Israel. In his farewell address several years later, Joshua warned the people: "If you turn away and ally yourselves with the survivors of these nations that remain among you and if you intermarry with them and associate with them, then you may be sure that the LORD your God will no longer drive out these nations before you. Instead, they will become snares and traps for you, whips on your backs and thorns in your eyes, until you perish from this good land, which the LORD your God has given you" (23:12–13). Sadly, this prediction came true. Time and again Israel would fall into the snares presented by those remaining nations.

But as for Caleb, he followed God wholeheartedly. For that faithfulness he was blessed with a long life, and he and his descendants received Hebron, the land God had promised to give him.

DISCUSSION

The golden years are a period of life in which some adults retire while others refire. While one adult settles into a rocking chair, another straps on a pair of hiking boots. Discuss if the golden years could bring new opportunities to stretch one's faith and attempt great things for God.

1. Read Joshua 14:5–12. How old was Caleb when he asked Joshua for his land inheritance?

2. How long had Caleb kept God's promise in his heart?

3. What commendable character traits do you find in Caleb as you read verses 6–12? Choose one of these traits and explain how you will implement it in your life.

4. If the Lord leaves you on earth until you are eighty-five, how do you hope to be serving Him then?

5. How might you show your children or grandchildren to wholeheartedly follow the Lord?

6. How do you know Caleb was aware of the huge challenges he faced in possessing the land promised to him?

PRAYER

Father, thank You that You always have exciting tasks ahead for us. Thank You for Your promises as we obey You. Help us to hear Your calling each and every day that we might faithfully follow.

RENEWING YOUR COVENANT WITH GOD

Joshua 24:14–27

Continually renew your covenant with God.

After being dismissed from the Korean Conflict by President Truman, General Douglas MacArthur addressed Congress. "Old soldiers never die," he said; "they just fade away." Centuries earlier, another old soldier addressed the nation of Israel, but his remarks were quite different. General Joshua had grown very old and was ready to die, but he would not simply fade away. He rehearsed God's mighty works on behalf of Israel, urged the nation to renew its covenant with the Lord, warned the nation about false gods, challenged everyone to choose whom they would serve, and confessed his and his family's commitment to serve the Lord.

This study challenges us to keep on serving the Lord until He calls us home.

COMMENTARY

Joshua was getting older, and the time of his death was coming near. Under Joshua's leadership much had been accomplished: (1) He led the Israelites into the Promised Land; (2) the land of Canaan had been conquered over a period of several years, and only pockets of the former nations remained; (3) Joshua divided up the land among the tribes, and eventually the land was further divided among the individual families within the tribes; (4) Levitical cities and cities of refuge had been designated; and (5) Reuben, Gad, and half the tribe of Manasseh had crossed back over the Jordan

River, returning to their allotment to the east of the river after helping in the conquest of the land west of the Jordan.

Before he died, Joshua assembled the leaders of Israel to give them final instructions. Also he warned them against marriages with people from the remaining nations and against alliances with those same people (Josh. 23). "Then Joshua assembled all the tribes of Israel at Shechem" (24:1). There Joshua cited the words of the Lord. He sketched a brief history of God's call to Abraham, Isaac, and Jacob and the subsequent deliverance from Egypt under Moses and Aaron. He reminded them of the victories over the Amorites east of the Jordan, and then the victories over Jericho and the various nations throughout the land of Canaan. "I sent the hornet ahead of you, which drove them out before you—also the two Amorite kings. You did not do it with your own sword and bow. So I gave you a land on which you did not toil and cities you did not build; and you live in them and eat from vineyards and olive groves that you did not plant" (24:12–13).

All this was in preparation for Joshua's final charge to the people, calling them to renew their covenant with the Lord. More than anything else he wanted the people he had successfully led for many years to remain faithful to the Lord. A renewed covenant between Israel and the Lord was a symbol of Joshua's hopes for them. The reminders he cited from their recent history were given to motivate them to reaffirm their allegiance to the Lord. Those victories proved that God had been faithful to keep His promises to them. Thus, as their parents in the previous generation before them had made a covenant under Moses, they agreed to renew the covenant with the Lord. Unfortunately, the future would show that the depth of their commitment was no greater than that of their parents. For their parents had soon broken their covenant with the Lord, disobeyed at Kadesh Barnea, and subsequently died in the wilderness during a forty-year period of wandering.

Now Fear the Lord and Serve Him with All Faithfulness (Josh. 24:14)

The Israelites had a problem being faithful. Idolatry remained a great snare for them throughout their history, at least until the time of the Babylonian exile. Only in that exile was idolatry finally purged from the people. Joshua recognized their weakness in the face of this temptation. He urged them to serve only the Lord. He wanted them to break away from the gods their forefathers had served back in Mesopotamia as well as the gods their parents had worshiped in Egypt. The Lord alone was worthy of their worship. The Lord was worthy not only because of who He was (is) but also because of what He had done for them in the miraculous events of the exodus from Egypt and the conquest of Canaan.

WORDS FROM WESLEY

Joshua 24:15

Trusting in the strength Divine
I vow to serve the Lord,
Christ shall be by me and mine
Acknowledged and adored:
Jesus, to my house and me
Now let Thy salvation come,
Now prepare our hearts to be
Thine everlasting home. (PW, vol. 9, 131)

But as for Me and My Household, We Will Serve the Lord (Josh. 24:15)

The choice was before them, and Joshua insisted that they choose: **"But if serving the LORD seems undesirable to you, then choose for yourselves this day whom you will serve, whether the gods your forefathers served beyond the River, or the gods of the Amorites, in whose land you are living"** (v. 15).

Joshua had already made his choice to serve the Lord. Now it was their turn, and he was doing all he could to force the issue as well as to influence them to make the right choice. The choice was seen as a group commitment for the people, not as an individual matter. Joshua chose for his family; they must choose for their families. On the other hand, it was also a matter of the heart, which surely is an individual decision.

Abraham had left the gods of his fathers beyond the Euphrates River. Moses had forsaken the gods of Egypt. Always the most important issue was related to the attitude of the heart. Moses had promised, "The LORD your God will circumcise your hearts and the hearts of your descendants, so that you may love him with all your heart and with all your soul, and live" (Deut. 30:6). Joshua wanted the hearts of his people to be devoted to the Lord in the same way his heart was devoted. He could plead with them and push them to serve the Lord, but ultimately in their hearts they had to decide whether to renew their covenant or not.

WORDS FROM WESLEY

Joshua 24:15

The worship of God is so highly reasonable, necessary and beneficial; and the service of idols so absurd, and vain, and pernicious, that if it were left free for all men to take their choice, every man in his right wits must needs chose the service of God, before that of idols; and provokes them to bind themselves faster to God by their own choice. *We will*—But know this, if you should all be so base and brutish, as to prefer senseless and impotent idols, before the true and living God, it is my firm purpose, that I will, and my children, and servants (as far as I can influence them) shall be constant and faithful to the Lord. And that, whatever others do. . . . They that are bound for heaven must be willing to swim against the stream, and must do, not as most do, but as the best do. (ENOT)

Then the People Answered, "Far Be It from Us to Forsake the Lord to Serve Other Gods!" (Josh. 24:16–18)

This was a point of high emotion after Joshua had reminded the Israelites of all God had done for them, and the people were ready to reaffirm their covenant with the Lord. It was obvious that God had supplied their needs abundantly and miraculously, delivering them, protecting them, and defeating their enemies time and again. How could they turn Him down after all He had done? They were ready to accept Joshua's challenge and make their choice for the Lord. Now they in turn recited the miraculous ways the Lord had provided for them. The Lord had delivered them from Egypt with miraculous signs, the Lord had protected them on their journey through hostile nations, and the Lord had driven out nations before them. So they affirmed, **"We too will serve the LORD, because he is our God"** (v. 18).

WORDS FROM WESLEY
Joshua 24:16

These words—That is, this covenant or agreement of the people with the Lord. *In the book*—That is, in the volume which was kept in the ark, Deut. 31:9, 26, whence it was taken and put into this book of Joshua: this he did for the perpetual remembrance of this great and solemn action, to lay the greater obligation upon the people to be true to their engagement; and as a witness for God, against the people, if afterward he punished them for their defection from God, to whom they had so solemnly and freely obliged themselves. (ENOT)

Joshua Said to the People, "You Are Not Able to Serve the Lord" (Josh. 24:19–20)

Joshua recognized that the reply of the people was quite casual, driven by the emotion of the moment. Instead, Joshua wanted a considered and heartfelt response; thus, he questioned their commitment. After all, their parents had been disobedient in the past, and if they continued that pattern of rebellion, the Lord would bring judgment on them. God had been good to them, but goodness could change to punishment. If they served other gods, disaster and destruction would come upon them. Joshua hoped they were more steadfast than their parents had been, but he well knew how fickle people could be.

WORDS FROM WESLEY
Joshua 24:19

The meaning is, God's service is not, as you seem to fancy, a slight and easy thing, but it is a work of great difficulty, and requires great care, and courage and resolution; and when I consider the infinite purity of God, that He will not be mocked or abused; and withal your proneness to superstition and idolatry, even during the life of Moses, and in some of you, while I live, and while the obligations which God had laid upon you in this land, are fresh in remembrance; I cannot but fear that after my decease you will think the service of God burdensome, and therefore will cast it off and revolt from Him, if you do not carefully avoid all occasions of idolatry. . . . *Will not forgive*—If you who own yourselves His people and servants, shall wilfully transgress His laws, He will not let this go unpunished in you, as He doth in other nations; . . . for as if you be sincere and faithful in God's service, you will have admirable benefits by it; so if you be false to your professions, and forsake Him whom you have so solemnly avouched to be your God, He will deal more severely with you than with any people in the world. (ENOT)

But the People Said to Joshua, "No! We Will Serve the Lord" (Josh. 24:21–22)

Unfazed by Joshua's challenge, the people strongly affirmed their loyalty to the Lord, and they pledged that they would serve Him. Joshua went on to point out that they themselves were witnesses to this promise and they would judge themselves if they failed to serve the Lord. To this all the people replied, **"Yes, we**

are witnesses" (v. 22). At that moment they certainly seemed to have neither reservations nor doubts.

"Now Then," Said Joshua, ". . . Yield Your Hearts to the Lord, the God of Israel" (Josh. 24:23–24)

Joshua pressed for more than just words to demonstrate that their promise was genuinely from their hearts. He asked them to take action to rid themselves of the foreign gods that were such a temptation to them. They should get rid of the source of the trouble by throwing those gods away. It was one thing for the Israelites to say they were committed; taking action was the way to show their commitment and demonstrate their resolve. Their commitment to the covenant was a matter of the heart, but actions often reveal better than words what is truly in the heart. Once again the people pledged: **"We will serve the LORD our God and obey him"** (v. 24). We are not told whether any gods actually ended up in the fire that night.

Joshua Made a Covenant for the People (Josh. 24:25–27)

Next Joshua formalized the promises of the people along with God's terms for the covenant by putting them in writing **in the Book of the Law of God** (v. 26). The record of the promises and the terms would be available for guidance and for future reference. If, indeed, the people were to be witnesses against themselves (24:22), then the record was needed for documentation.

Joshua also made a visible and physical expression of their covenant: **Then he took a large stone and set it up there under the oak near the holy place of the LORD. "See!" he said to all the people. "This stone will be a witness against us. It has heard all the words the LORD has said to us. It will be a witness against you if you are untrue to your God"** (vv. 26–27). The use of stones as reminders of important events was common among the Israelites. Several memorials were set up in the conquest of Canaan, and those memorials helped the people remember God's acts on their behalf. This particular stone at Shechem was to be a continual reminder of the covenant Israel had renewed with the Lord under Joshua to encourage their faithfulness. If they failed to keep their covenant, it was to be a continual rebuke to their sins.

After setting up the memorial, Joshua had done all he could to help shape the future course of events for Israel. He had reminded the people of God's miraculous providence in calling the patriarchs and in bringing Israel out of Egypt and into the Promised Land. He had challenged them to make their choice whether or not to serve the Lord. He had warned them of the consequences they would face if they rebelled. He had written down the terms of the covenant. And he had set up a visible reminder for them. The most important part—the inner work on their hearts—was beyond Joshua's reach. The people had to make their choice, and only then could God "circumcise their hearts."

DISCUSSION

Occasionally citizens of the United States recite the Pledge of Allegiance. It is good to do so often and with heartfelt loyalty. Discuss when believers need to renew their "pledge of allegiance" to God occasionally and do so with heartfelt loyalty.

1. What three responsibilities did Joshua give the Israelites in Joshua 24:14?

2. If you were to grade your own past faithfulness to the Lord, what letter would you assign? Why?

3. Why do you agree or disagree that idolatry may occupy a place in the hearts of Christians?

4. What choice did Joshua offer the Israelites? Do believers today have this choice? Why or why not?

5. Joshua assumed spiritual leadership for his household (v. 15). Should the father assume spiritual leadership for his household today? If so, what specific challenges to this leadership might he encounter?

6. In what sense is God "jealous" (v. 19)?

7. How did the Israelites show they would renew their covenant with the Lord?

8. Do you need to throw away any "gods" as you yield your heart to the Lord (v. 23)? If so, what gods will you throw away today?

PRAYER

Father, we want to serve You and You alone. Show us where there are idols in our lives and forgive us for our unfaithfulness to You.

WHAT ABOUT THE NEXT GENERATION?

Judges 2:6–23

Every generation needs to know God and His redemption.

How much longer will freedom reign in Western nations? Doesn't it seem that religious liberty is slipping away from both Canada and the United States as each government imposes restrictions on when, where, and how Christian practices may be observed? If we continue on this slippery slope away from God and absolute truth, soon we may resemble the Israelites in the times of the judges. In those days, everyone did what was right in their own eyes, and God responded by allowing Israel's enemies to oppress the nation until the people repented. Deliverance came only when Israel repented and turned back to God.

This study raises warning flags and summons us to remain loyal to God.

COMMENTARY

The book of Judges has two introductory sections: 1:1—2:5 and 2:6—3:6, and the two are not in chronological sequence. The starting point of 1:1 is "after the death of Joshua," while 2:6 begins during his life. If placed chronologically, 1:1—2:5 would be inserted between 2:6–9 and 2:10 as it recounts events of the generation that outlived Joshua but prior to the period of the judges.

The first introductory section is more historical; it deals with the continued military conquest of the land. The thematic movement is the "lack of conquest" as it recounts the decline of the Israelites' superiority over the Canaanites in the attempts to drive the Canaanites from the land. It concludes with a theological indictment that explains the lack of continued conquest.

The second introductory section is more theological; it provides the framework through which the particular accounts of the judges that follow in 3:7 through chapter 16 are to be understood.

From Joshua to the Judges (Judg. 2:6–10)

Whereas Judges 2:6 begins by referring to the covenant ceremony during the time of Joshua, verse 7 moves ahead to those who outlived Joshua. That generation is characterized as both serving the Lord and as having **seen all the great things the LORD had done for Israel** (v. 7). Those **great things** involved the divine protection and provision during the years in the wilderness, the defeat of the Transjordan kings, the crossing of the Jordan River, and the conquests under Joshua. Verses 8–9, quoting Joshua 24:29–30, recount the death and burial of Joshua.

The chronological transition continues in 2:10 as it recounts the rise of the subsequent generation. This new generation is contrasted with the preceding one of verse 7. The preceding one had **served the LORD** (v. 7) and seen God's mighty works on their behalf, whereas the new generation **knew neither the LORD nor what he had done for Israel** (v. 10). From Judges 1:1—2:5, it is evident that the mighty workings of God were declining as the previous generation failed to do what the LORD had intended them to do with respect to driving out the Canaanites, so the chance of this new generation's seeing such things had also diminished. But this new generation was clearly held responsible for not knowing the Lord. So 2:6–10 is a transition from the faithful generation during the time of Joshua, and just subsequent to his death, to the new generation, which lacked commitment to the Lord.

People's Action: Apostasy Provokes the Lord to Anger (Judg. 2:11–13)

The new generation turned away from the Lord and went after other gods. Several passages in Deuteronomy (4:25; 9:18; 31:29) show that the opening phrase (**the Israelites did evil in the eyes of the LORD** [2:11]) plus **they provoked the LORD to anger** (v. 12) were a stereotypical combination. Likewise here, those two phrases form the thesis statement of verses 11–13, with the former being the general accusation and the latter being the evoked result.

The other phrases in verses 11–13 are the specific elaboration of what the evil was. The accusation here in verses 11–13 was not some superficial disobedience about external matters of proper ritual worship or behavior, but was rebellion against the Lord. The forsaking of the Lord and going after other gods was the supreme breach of the covenant relationship because it violated the first commandment of having no other God besides the Lord. And since the Baals and Ashtoreths were idols, the worship of them inevitably led to a violation of the second commandment of not having any carved images.

WORDS FROM WESLEY
Judges 2:11

In the sight—Which notes the heinousness and impudence of their sins, above other peoples; because God's presence was with them, and His eye upon them in a peculiar manner, which also they were not ignorant of, and therefore were guilty of more contempt of God than other people. (ENOT)

Divine Response: Sending Enemies Who Oppress the Israelites (Judg. 2:14–16)

The divine response to the people's apostasy was that the anger of the Lord was expressed against them (**in his anger against**

Israel the LORD [v. 14]) in the form of oppressing them through their enemies. The Lord actively did three things: He **handed them over to raiders; he sold them to their enemies;** and **the hand of the LORD was against them to defeat them** (vv. 14–15). The Israelites came under the afflicting hands of both the Lord and their enemies, which worked in a coordinated way against the Israelites.

Verses 14–15 express three results deriving from the divine action. First, verse 14 gives the result inflicted on the Israelites: the enemies, in sporadic incursions, **plundered them.**

Second is the shift to the consequential situations in which the Israelites found themselves: their military powerlessness to stand against the enemies and the chronic condition of being in dire straits both physically and psychologically.

Third is that the judgment the Lord was carrying out was that which He said He would do (**just as he had sworn to them** [v. 15]). Previously, in Joshua 24:20, Joshua had specifically warned the people, "If you forsake the LORD and serve foreign gods, he will turn and bring disaster [evil] on you." That warning is based on the covenant curses for disobedience in Deuteronomy 28:15–68. The fact that the Lord was doing what He had previously sworn to do emphasizes God's faithfulness to the covenant, even when it meant acting in judgment against disobedience.

WORDS FROM WESLEY

Judges 2:16

Raised up—By inward inspiration and excitation of their hearts, and by outward designation testified by some extraordinary action. *Judges*—Supreme magistrates, whose office it was, under God, and by His particular direction, to govern the commonwealth of Israel by God's laws, and to protect and save them from their enemies, to preserve and purge religion, and to maintain the liberties of the people against all oppressors. (ENOT)

People's Action: Groaning in Their Affliction Moves the Lord to Change (Judg. 2:18)

Although stressed in the subsequent narratives through the phrase "and the Israelites cried out to the Lord," this aspect of the pattern is only referred to in verse 18: **the Lord had compassion on them as they groaned under those who oppressed and afflicted them**. The language here in verse 18 makes the comparison between the people's current situation and the oppression they experienced in Egypt. Not only is the term **afflicted** used to describe the Egyptian oppression (compare Ex. 3:9), but the term **groaned** is used only three other times, two of which occur in Exodus. There, the people groaned under the slavery, to which the Lord responded by delivering them (Ex. 2:24; 6:5). Just as the Lord responded to their cries for help while in Egypt, so too the Lord responded to their cries of help in the current oppression and sent a deliverer.

The result of the people's plea for help was a moving of the Lord to have **compassion on them** (Judg. 2:18). The effect of the people's groaning was that the Lord had a change of mind, which motivated Him to alter what He was doing or causing to happen. Verse 18 affirms that the Lord responded to the people's situation: just as the people's sin provoked the Lord to anger (v. 12), so now the people's cries for help motivated the Lord to alter the course of action He was taking against them so that He delivered them.

WORDS FROM WESLEY

Judges 2:18

It repented the Lord—That is, the Lord changed His course and dealings with them, as penitent men use to do; removed His judgements, and returned to them in mercy. (ENOT)

Divine Action: Raising Up of Judges Who Deliver the Israelites (Judg. 2:16–19)

The generation that inaugurated the period of the judges was described in verses 10–13. But in verse 17, the negative character of the generations during the judges is amplified even further through the addition of new accusations. First, **they would not listen to their judges** (v. 17). The people's lack of listening to the Lord (v. 20) was mirrored in their lack of listening to the divinely appointed human leaders.

Second, in the description of going after other gods, there is the repetition from verse 12 that they **worshiped them,** but there is the new aspect that they **prostituted themselves to other gods** (v. 17). Prostituting oneself is used metaphorically to liken the people's spiritual infidelity to sexual promiscuity. Its use as a metaphor to describe going after other gods seems apropos given that some of the worship practices related to those pagan fertility deities involved erotic rituals.

The third accusation is made through a contrast with the previous generation, that this generation had **quickly turned from the way . . . of obedience to the LORD's commands** (v. 17), thus not walking in the way of their ancestors. This generation continued to be as it was described in verses 10–13, in contrast to **their fathers** (v. 17), whose obedience is described in verse 7. The language here alludes to the golden calf incident, where occurs the only other use of the expression "quickly turned away" (Ex. 32:8; Deut. 9:12, 16). This generation is like that one who, a mere forty days after having entered into covenant with the Lord, became involved in idolatrous worship.

In Judges 2:19, with respect to the period after each particular judge died, the three sins that are specified (**following other gods and serving and worshiping them**) are all repeated from verses 11–13. Yet what is stressed in verse 19 is an intensification of the sin committed by each successive generation, with their ways being even more corrupt than those of their fathers. Whereas in verse 17, **their fathers** is a reference to the previous faithful generation of verse 7, here in verse 19, **their fathers** refers to the previous unfaithful generation of verses 10–17. The people's actions were motivated by a recalcitrant spirit of refusal **to give up their evil practices and stubborn ways** (v. 19). The use of the term **ways** in both verses 17 and 19 helps to highlight the contrast again between the **way of obedience to the LORD's commands** (v. 17) and its opposite, the people's **stubborn ways** (v. 19).

WORDS FROM WESLEY

Judges 2:19

Returned—To their former, and usual course. *Their fathers*—In Egypt, or in the wilderness. *Their own doings*—That is, from their evil practices, which he calls their own, because they were agreeable to their own natures, which in all mankind are deeply and universally corrupted, and because they were familiar and customary to them. (ENOT)

Further Consequence: Nations Left in the Land (Judg. 2:20–23)

Verses 20–22 are a divine declaration in the form of an announcement of judgment, which has three parts: (1) the reason for the judgment is given in verse 20; (2) the declaration of the judgment is given in verses 21–22; and (3) the redemptive purpose of the judgment is stated in verse 22.

As the Lord began His indictment to Israel in verse 20, He called them **this nation**, which gives a sense of the Lord distancing himself from His people. The indictment was expressed in general terms of the people's having **violated the covenant** and **not listened to** the Lord (v. 20). The indictment was generically that of disobedience, which involved a broad spectrum of transgressions.

The judgment was given in verse 21: the Lord would **no longer drive out before them any of the nations**. Prior to entering the land, in Joshua 1:2–9, God had promised to give His people complete victory in driving out the people of the land. But He had based the success of such on the people's obedience to the covenant law. The judgment here made it clear that the people's lack of obedience had negated the fulfillment of the promise regarding the land. Neither the covenant nor the promises were ultimately voided by the people's disobedience; rather that generation did not realize the fulfillment of the promises.

Whereas in 1:1—2:5, there had been a decline in the "conquest" of the enemies in the land; with this judgment in 2:21, the Lord declared that there would not be any further conquest at all. The fulfillment of this judgment is implicit in the subsequent narratives in which the judges only deal with gaining relief from the enemies' oppression, but are not involved in any way in taking over enemy-held territory allotted to Israel.

In verse 22, however, the Lord declared that even this judgment had a redemptive purpose: **I will use them to test Israel**. The point of this test is to **see whether they will keep the way of the LORD and walk in it** (v. 22; compare 3:4). Such a test is to be distinguished from any form of tempting to lure someone to do wrong. Whereas a temptation arises out of the desire to have the people fail or fall away, the purpose of a test arises out of the desire for the people to prove themselves loyal. In this case, God's desire was that the people would pass the test by remaining faithful to Him and not go after the gods of the nations.

DISCUSSION

Joshua led the Israelites to renew their covenant with the Lord, but soon after, he died. Discuss what became of the next generation.

1. What alarming contrast do you find in Judges 2:6–11?

2. What words come to mind to describe what life would be like if everyone ignored laws and did what was right in his or her own eyes?

3. Why do you agree or disagree that a congregation reaches a critical juncture when a godly pastor retires, passes away, or becomes the pastor of another church?

4. What cycle do you see repeated in verses 10–19?

5. Why do you agree or disagree that any "Christian" nation that declines spiritually puts itself at risk of being subdued by its enemies?

6. What happened in Canaan because the Israelites violated God's covenant (vv. 20–23)?

7. How would you differentiate "freedom of religion" from "freedom from religion"?

8. How would you define "separation of church and state"?

9. Although neither the United States nor Canada is in a covenant relationship with God, what principles for national security can you draw from Joshua 2:6–23?

PRAYER

Father, although we cannot make the decision of faith for anyone else, You call us to share about You and Your works to the next generation. Please give us wisdom, creativity, and opportunity to do so.

8

GODLY LEADERSHIP

Judges 4:4–16

God selects and equips people to be His leaders.

One might wonder how churches would function without the contribution of godly women. They usually outnumber men as Sunday school teachers, nursery attendants, visitation workers, and choir members. They often give their time and talent to the Lord on behalf of others without expecting any praise. Missionary work, too, often moves forward because dedicated women serve as teachers, nurses, directors of orphanages, and musicians. In many facets of missionary work, they serve where there are no male missionaries. Their commitment and compassion are exemplary.

This study spotlights Deborah, a female judge and brave military leader, and it instills gratitude in us for godly women who serve the Lord.

COMMENTARY

The book of Judges chronicles the Israelites' struggle to conquer Canaan, both the land and the religion. The story is a cycle of divine deliverance, human disobedience, divine punishment, human repentance, and divine deliverance. The Israelites always seemed outnumbered and seemed to lack the confidence for victory. Repeatedly, the writer of Judges recorded that the Lord went before the military and secured its victory. The men merely needed to do as God commanded. With that sort of confidence, it is an intriguing story to see how quickly the Israelites forgot their God and accepted the foreign teachings of the Canaanite religion.

Also within that cycle is the tragic story of an ever-increasing level of sin within the Israelite people. With each passing judge, the people did more evil in the sight of the Lord than their fathers. Successive judges received less support and more resistance from the people. In the end, Samson, the last judge, was as much a representation of the sinful people as he was a representation of the salvation of God. In fact, the summary of Samson's reign bears no mention of peace in the land while he lived (Judg. 16:31).

Historically, this story occurred at the end of the Bronze Age and beginning of the Iron Age, roughly 1200 B.C. The iron chariots in Judges 4:3 had iron fittings. They were not made exclusively of iron or they would have been too heavy to move. The Israelites were slow to adapt iron works, so the Canaanite iron chariots were a formidable force to face. This is interesting since the battle happened in the plains, and the Israelites led by Deborah lived in the hill country out of reach of Sisera's chariots. The Israelites intentionally engaged their oppressor.

So another contextual aspect is power. This story explicitly shows the power of God superior to the power of humanity, and the power of faith superior to the power of oppression. Even though power is a constant struggle in the human experience, it was a special concern during this time when power shifted quickly and often between embattled cities and self-proclaimed rulers "of the four corners of the earth." Political intrigue was intense, fueled by extensive intelligence networks and ever-changing alliances. Note that Jabin "reigned in Hazor," but his army commander "lived in Harosheth Haggoyim" (4:2). This relationship was defined and maintained carefully. It was Sisera's defeat that signaled Jabin's demise (4:23–24). Power was truly precarious.

In one particular way, the story of the Judges is a precursor to the story of Jesus. "Whenever the LORD raised up a judge for them, he was with the judge and saved them out of the hands of their enemies as long as the judge lived; for the LORD has compassion on them as they groaned under those who oppressed and afflicted them" (2:18). That is, the judge was a type of incarnation, though a temporary one. "But when the judge died, the people returned to ways even more corrupt than their fathers" (2:19). As long as there was a living presence of God among them, the Israelites did not deny their God, but without the judge, "everyone did as he saw fit" (21:25).

Deborah and Her Authority (Judg. 4:4–6)

Deborah's authority spanned all aspects of life—religious, civil, and military. The first thing we learn about **Deborah** is that she was **a prophetess** (v. 4). Despite the modern view of prophecy as foretelling the future, the biblical understanding of prophecy is the utterance of divine words. In the Old Testament, a prophet (or prophetess) was not necessarily a priest. (Later God used prophets to rebuke the priesthood.) So the most important thing the title **prophetess** conveys is that Deborah possessed a personal relationship with God. It was from this relationship that her power was derived. This differs significantly from Israel's neighbors in Canaan. Other people considered their leaders not only divinely appointed, but divine themselves. But the task of the prophetess was to mediate the relationship between God and the people as a divine mouthpiece and human exemplar. It is interesting to note that the title "prophet" is not associated with any other judge.

Next, we are introduced to Deborah's husband. We can assume he was an important man simply because he is mentioned in the text. Also telling is the description of **Deborah** as **the wife of Lappidoth** (v. 4) such that the reader was expected to know that name even if Deborah was somehow unknown.

Third, we see Deborah as the judge of Israel. At this time, Israel was governed by tribal clans. There was no king or centralized government. The rest of the region was dominated by city-states with periodic "dynasties" rising to control several cities for relatively short times. However, the biblical precedent, at least since Moses, was for God to appoint a divine speaker to judge civil life according to divine principles. The cases heard by Deborah would be those too difficult for tribal tribunes. She was something like the Supreme Court of Israel.

That **she held court under the Palm of Deborah** (v. 5) may suggest she owned land. It may be that the palm was named after her, that the land was her inheritance, or that the palm had been named after one of her ancestors. The palm usually denotes peace in the Bible. This would be fitting in here due to the association of peace with the lives of the early judges (see 3:11, 30; 5:31).

Finally, we see Deborah's authority extended over the military. However, her military authority rested on her role as a prophetess. **"The LORD, the God of Israel, commands you"** (v. 6), she told Barak. We are not told what Barak's military experience was, but we may assume he had some. Israel did not have a standing army at this time. It operated on the militia principle. So any military authority was occasional; that is, the authority existed only as long as the battle or war was fought. Afterward, the fighting men returned to their families, farms, and trades. This system was well fitted for the office of the prophet, which was also occasional in that the prophet did not receive a constant stream of communication from God, but rather received messages that were time sensitive and historically centered. So Deborah did not call Barak on her own authority, but in response to God's word given to Deborah.

All in all, we see in Deborah a person with whom God was intimate. This intimacy manifested itself in authority among her people. Her gender did not seem to be a factor. God did not seem to call her because she was a woman or because no man was fit to lead. We are not told why she was called. We are given a picture of faith, intimacy, and power that transcends human understanding and invites us into the mind of God.

WORDS FROM WESLEY

Judges 4:6

Called Barak—By virtue of that power which God had given her, and the people owned in her. *Kedesh Naphtali*—So called, to distinguish it from other places of that name, one in Judah, and another in Issachar. *Hath not the Lord*—That is, assuredly God hath commanded thee; this is not the fancy of a weak woman, which peradventure thou mayst despise; but the command of the great God by my mouth. (ENOT)

Preparing for Battle (Judg. 4:6–13)

From a militaristic viewpoint, the Israelites had no preparation for this battle. Barak garnered **ten thousand** militia **men** (v. 6) and took a position on the high ground, out of the reach of Sisera's chariots. Then he waited. Before we judge Barak too harshly, we must understand what he understood.

WORDS FROM WESLEY

Judges 4:8

I will not go—His offer to go with her, shows the truth of his faith, for which he is praised, Heb. 11:32, but his refusal to go without her, shows the weakness of his faith, that he could not trust God's bare word, as he ought to have done, without the pledge of the presence of his prophetess. (ENOT)

Sisera had extensive military preparation. He had a standing army that included **nine hundred iron chariots** (v. 13). These chariots carried two, possibly three, soldiers each, plus extra weapons. Sisera also had a spy, **Heber the Kenite** (v. 11), who used to have an alliance with Israel. Heber positioned himself between the city of Jabin and the city of Sisera. Since trade was so important, this was probably a primary economic alliance.

Probably Harosheth Haggoyim was a valuable trading port, and as such was subject to frequent attacks. Sisera would have defended it before; therefore, he would have had some idea of his battle plan. The story presents Sisera as confidently taking up his position.

The key to preparation for the Israelites was faith. God declared that He would lure Sisera, his chariots, and his army into a vulnerable position, and He would give the Israelites the victory. Barak believed that his God was strong, but he did not understand the personal nature of his God. Barak's mistake was that he treated Deborah like an idol. Armies carried the idols of their gods into battle as talismans. Barak considered Deborah a talisman. He lacked the personal knowledge of God that Deborah had. Barak believed he would win if Deborah were with him because he considered her presence proof of God's presence. Interestingly, Hebrews chapter 11 begins, "Now faith is being sure of what we hope for and certain of what we do not see." However, it is Barak, not Deborah, who is listed in 11:32 as extolling this virtue.

Deborah agreed to go with Barak in a matter-of-fact manner, suggesting she had prior knowledge of Barak's reaction. We need not see the Lord's decision as retribution against Barak as much as it is the logical result of Barak's actions. God promised Barak strength. Barak chose the weaker way, thinking it was the stronger way. So God used what Barak thought was weakness to defeat what Barak thought might be undefeatable.

We must not make the mistake of arguing from the particular to the general so that we see in this story a biblical assertion that women are weaker than men. It is true that men generally posses greater muscular strength than women. It is also true that women were not considered equal to men in most ancient societies. However, this does not constitute a general principle of female subordination. In fact, this story may illustrate the opposite. God uses what society deems weak to defeat what society reveres as strong. Women are not inherently weak. Men are not inherently strong. The issue is faith. While Heber broke his alliance with Israel (an unfaithful act), his wife, Jael, remained faithful. The moral of the story is this: "Trust in the LORD with all your heart and lean not on your own understanding; in all your ways acknowledge him, and he will make your paths straight" (Prov. 3:5–6).

The Battle (Judg. 4:14–16)

After building the anticipation and setting out the tensions, the battle itself is described simply and briefly. The important points are not how the men were strategically placed or how the chariots became impotent. The vital question is the rhetorical, **"Has not the LORD gone ahead of you?"** (v. 14).

●

WORDS FROM WESLEY

Judges 4:14

Up—Heb. arise, delay not. If we have ground to believe, that God goes before us, we may well go on with courage and cheerfulness. *Gone before thee*—Namely, as general of thine army, to fight for thee. *Went down*—He doth not make use of the advantage which he had of the hill, where he might have been out of the reach of his iron chariots, but boldly marcheth down into the valley, to give Sisera the opportunity of using all his horses and chariots, that so the victory might be more glorious. (ENOT)

From the resounding yes came two results. First, Sisera abandoned the chariots in which he had placed all his confidence and security. Note the absence of the adjective *iron* in verse 15 that was present in verse 13. The powerful iron chariots were now objects of derision, no longer evoking fear.

WORDS FROM WESLEY

Judges 4:15

Discomfited—With great terror and noise, as the word signifies, probably with thunder and lightning, and hail-stones, poured upon them from heaven, as is implied, chap. 5:20. *Edge of the sword*—That is, by the sword of Barak and his army, whose ministry God used; but so, that they had little else to do, but to kill those whom God by more powerful arms had put to flight. *On his feet*—That he might flee away more secretly in the quality of a common soldier, whereas his chariot would have exposed him to more observation. (ENOT)

Second, Barak continued the pursuit, giving hope that the Israelites might yet conquer the Canaanites. He continued to pursue the enemy back to its source and utterly destroyed it. This is where Israel had failed in the past, refusing to destroy the enemies of God.

Ultimately, the victory came from the recurring biblical motif of the day of the Lord." In verse 14, Deborah shouted, **"Go! This is the day the LORD has given Sisera into your hands."** On this day, judgment came to God's enemies and salvation came to His people. That is the essence of the day of the Lord. The day the world knows that it lives not by might nor by power, but by the Spirit of the Lord Almighty (Zech. 4:6).

DISCUSSION

Some nations have assigned the highest office in the land to a woman and then applauded her as a strong, wise, capable leader. Discuss what happened centuries ago when a woman became a leader in Israel and a powerful enemy oppressed the nation.

1. What leadership roles did Deborah fill according to Judges 4:4?

2. How has a Christian woman exerted an outstanding influence in your life?

3. Based on his response to Deborah (see vv. 6–8), what is your first impression of Barak?

4. How did Deborah respond to Barak?

5. How did she encourage him for battle (v. 14)?

6. What admirable qualities do you see in Barak?

7. How does the Lord's victory over Sisera encourage you?

8. In what circumstances has the Lord achieved a great victory for you?

PRAYER

Father, You go before us to defeat our enemies. Teach us to run to the battle with great confidence.

9

THE BATTLE BELONGS TO THE LORD

Judges 7:1–8, 19–21

The power for victory comes from God.

A Scottish pastor was criticized by his board because only one soul had accepted Christ during the fiscal year: Bobby Moffat. Little did anyone know at the time that Bobby Moffat would eventually become a missionary to Africa, where he would open mission stations in the interior and translate the Bible into the language of the Bechuanas. But then, God delights to use ordinary people to do extraordinary things. God used Gideon, a peasant farmer, and three hundred poorly armed men to defeat the vast numbers of Midianite invaders.

This study inspires confidence in God's unrivaled wisdom and power.

COMMENTARY

The story of Gideon in Judges 6–8 follows the pattern of apostasy to oppression to crying out (groaning) to deliverance established in 2:11–19. The details of the story are filled in more than any of the three preceding accounts. Thus it gives a much more vivid description of the oppression caused by the marauding Midianites, Amalekites, and other eastern peoples. In response to the people's crying out, the Lord sent a prophet to explain the reason for the oppression. The Lord appeared to Gideon, calling and commissioning him to deliver the people. But first, the Lord commanded Gideon to tear down the family and city altar to Baal and cut down the accompanying Asherah pole (6:25–32).

The Setting and Location (Judg. 7:1)

The Midianites were a seminomadic people from that region. The Amalekites were also a nomadic type people. The "eastern peoples" seems to be a generic description of other various nomadic tribes from the Transjordan. Throughout chapter 7, the enemy is simply referred to as "Midian," "the Midianites," or "the camp of Midian," which is an inclusive term and does not mean that the Israelites fought only one of these people groups in the battle.

The Midianite camp was located **near the hill of Moreh** (modern Nebi Dahi), lying about four miles north of **the Spring of Harod** (En Harod) at the base of Mount Gilboa, where Gideon's men were. They were encamped some three miles directly east of Gideon's hometown. As the scene began, the Israelite forces were outnumbered at least four to one.

Reduction in the Israelite Forces (Judg. 7:2–8)

Even though Gideon was seriously outnumbered, the Lord told him he had **"too many men for me to deliver Midian into their hands"** (v. 2). The Lord recognized the potential within the people to take credit for a victory (see Deut. 8:11–18). To demonstrate beyond a doubt that it was not the people's achievement, the military force would be pared down to the point that any victory achieved must be considered a miracle granted by the Lord.

WORDS FROM WESLEY

Judges 7:2

Too many—For my purpose; which is, so to deliver Israel, that it may appear to be my own act, that so I may have all the glory, and they may be the more strongly obliged to serve me. This may help us to understand those providences, which sometimes seem to weaken the church of Christ. Its friends are too many, too mighty, too wise, for God to work deliverance by. God is taking a course to lessen them, that He may be exalted in His own strength. (ENOT)

The reduction of the army occurred in two stages. The first allowed those who were afraid to leave: **"Anyone who trembles with fear may turn back and leave Mount Gilead"** (Judg. 7:3). Fear on the part of Israelite soldiers was evidence of a lack of trust in the divine presence and promises. When Gideon's forces were so challenged, almost 70 percent of them left the battle area: **So twenty-two thousand men left, while ten thousand remained** (v. 3). But the irony is that Gideon was still afraid (vv. 10–11); when those who were afraid were asked to leave, perhaps Gideon should have been among them!

Left with ten thousand men, Gideon must have been further disconcerted when the Lord told him, **"There are still too many men"** (v. 4) and went through a second process of reducing the number of troops (vv. 4–6). The Lord said: **"I will sift them for you there. If I say, 'This one shall go with you,' he shall go; but if I say, 'This one shall not go with you,' he shall not go"** (v. 4). Since the conditions in verse 5 was revealed only to Gideon (**the LORD told him**), the men were totally unaware of the criterion, and probably even that they were being evaluated.

Once the fighting force had been pared down by another 97 percent, leaving less than 1 percent of the original fighting force, the Lord again gave the promise to Gideon that He would give the victory: **"I will save you and give the Midianites into your hands"** (v. 7).

To Gideon's credit, he did not question the Lord in this process, but was fully obedient to what the Lord told him to do. When commanded in verse 4, **"Take them down to the water,"** verse 5 tells us, **so Gideon took the men down to the water**. When God told him, with respect to the ninety-seven hundred men, **"Let all the other men go, each to his own place"** (v. 7), **Gideon sent the rest of the Israelites to their tents** (v. 8). Regardless of what Gideon was feeling internally at that point, he was faithful to what the Lord commanded him to do.

●

WORDS FROM WESLEY
Judges 7:7

His own place—That is, to his own home. By this farther distinction it was proved, that none should be made use of, but (1) men that were hardy, that could endure fatigue, without complaining of thirst or weariness; (2) men that were hasty, that thought it long, 'till they were engaged with the enemy, and so just wetted their mouth and away, not staying for a full draught. Such as these God chose to employ, that are not only well affected, but zealously affected to His work. (ENOT)

The Israelites Executing the Battle Plan (Judg. 7:19–21)

We are not told where Gideon's battle plan came from; there is no reference to it being given directly to him by the Lord. Such stands out in light of the Lord's repeated direct communications with Gideon in verses 2, 4–5, and 7. The silence may indicate that the plan was not explicitly communicated to him, but developed by Gideon through using godly wisdom, which is an equally valid way of following God when there is no explicit new divine directive. It may be that the plan had been preformulated, since in verse 8 the acquiring of the "provisions and trumpets" from the others before they left seems to already anticipate the need of those items in the coming battle. Although "provisions" can refer to supplies and food in a general sense, in this case it is probably more specific, synonymous with "utensils," thus including the jars used in verses 16 and 19–20.

The plan was executed just as Gideon had laid it out (7:16–18). The three hundred men were divided into three companies and stationed at three different locations around the Midianite camp at its very **edge** (v. 19). All of the three hundred men had **trumpets**, literally a ram's horn (*shofar*) as opposed to a metal trumpet. The different blasts of the ram's horn trumpets were used to direct the troops in battle (see 2 Sam. 18:16; Neh. 4:18–20), and thus normally each soldier would not have one, but only those directing the troop movements. They each also had **torches**, whose flames were concealed in empty pottery **jars** that could be easily broken (Judg. 7:20).

WORDS FROM WESLEY

Judges 7:18

What power against a worm can stand
Arm'd with Jehovah's sword?
And all who bow to Christ's command
Are champions of the Lord!
Arm'd with His word and Spirit's might
We shall the battle gain,
And sin, that tempting Midianite,
Shall be for ever slain. (PW, vol. 9, 135–136)

The "attack" took place **at the beginning of the middle** of the night **watch** (v. 19). Assuming that the night was broken into three watches (8 p.m. to midnight, midnight to 4 a.m., 4 to 8 a.m.), such would be around midnight. It occurred **just after they had changed the guard** (v. 19), at a point when there would still have been some movement in the camp, which would have made the movements of the Israelites less detectable.

When Gideon's company **blew their trumpets and broke the jars** (v. 19), the other two companies immediately joined in (v. 20). That was followed by the war cry going up: **"A sword for the LORD and for Gideon!"** (v. 20).

The silence of the night was shattered by the repeated blaring of the horns, the unison breaking of the jars, and the repeated shouting of the war cry. The darkness of the night was shattered by the light from the torches. Because it was nighttime—with the majority of the Midianites asleep—in the stupor of their rude awakening, they probably assumed that the multiplicity of horns being blown and the brightness of the many torches meant the Israelites were still at their original level of strength. And the war cry that spoke of the sword suggested that the Israelites had their weapons fully drawn and were attacking the fringes of the camp. But it is clear that the "battle" strategy was intended to create a ruse and a ruckus that would produce panic among the Midianites, and probably stampede their camels, rather than being a strategy of fighting. With the **torches in their left hands and holding in their right hands the trumpets** (v. 20), they had no free hands with which they could wield any weapons. Also, the Israelites did not invade the Midian camp, rather **each man held his position around the camp** (v. 21).

The Result of the Israelites' and the Lord's Actions (Judg. 7:21)

In the midst of the Israelites' "nighttime serenade," verse 21 recounts that **all the Midianites ran, crying out as they fled**. Because **ran** and **fled** seem redundant, **ran** may have the connotation of "jumping up"—the first reaction they had when the noise disrupted their sleep (see Ps. 18:29; Joel 2:9, where it means "leaping" or "scaling" walls). The Midianites were thrown into a panicked, hysterical flight. But beyond just fleeing from the camp without casualties, verse 22 recounts the other thing that happened. Here the narrator did precisely what the Lord intended in verse 2, in that the result was directly attributed to the Lord. It was the Lord who gave the victory by causing the Midianites to turn on themselves, slaying one another (see 2 Chron. 20:23). Whereas the Israelites had shouted, "A sword for the LORD and for Gideon!" (Judg. 7:20), they did not actually wield a sword in the fight. Rather the only swords mentioned were those of the Midianites'—used by the Lord, and turned against themselves.

The casualty statistic for the Midianites is reserved for later in the narrative in 8:10: 120,000 "swordsmen" (note the reference to "sword" again) died in the self-slaughter and the Israelites' initial pursuit of the army—a casualty rate of 89 percent. And more died in the subsequent pursuit by Gideon (8:11–12). An impressive victory indeed, considering the three hundred Israelites did not initially fight, but stood around playing instruments (vv. 21–22)!

WORDS FROM WESLEY

Judges 7:22

Against his fellow—They slew one another, because they suspected treachery, and so fell upon those they first met with; which they might more easily do, because they consisted of several nations, because the darkness of the night made them unable to distinguish friends from foes, because the suddenness of the thing struck them with horror and amazement; and because God had infatuated them, as He had done many others. (ENOT)

DISCUSSION

When the Midianites invaded Israel, they and their allies settled into position as thick as locusts. The Israelites, under the leadership of Gideon, were able to draft thirty-two thousand soldiers, but the Lord dismissed all but three hundred of them.

1. According to Judges 7:2, what danger was inherent in Gideon having an army of thirty-two thousand?

2. Of the thirty-two thousand, how many were stricken with fear and sent home?

3. What important military trait did the three hundred who lapped water like a dog possess?

4. Why do you agree or disagree that confidence in numbers may weaken a church?

5. Why do you agree or disagree that a small church may hold back God's power by thinking it is too small to make a difference?

6. Read Judges 7:19–21. How might believers today defeat the Enemy by sounding a trumpet and shining their light?

PRAYER

Father, You work in unexpected ways; Your methods are not ours. Help us to trust You to win the battle when we don't have the resources. And help us to always obey You, with complete confidence in Your ultimate plan.

10

FAILURE IS NOT FINAL

Judges 13:2–5; 16:23–31

God is able to equip and use those whom He calls,
even after they fail.

The book of Judges reports astounding exploits of strength demonstrated by Samson when the Spirit of the Lord came upon him. Although some misinformed individuals attribute Samson's amazing strength to his long hair, his hair was simply a sign of his separation to God. Sadly, Samson's sinning left him weak, humiliated, and incarcerated.

This study emphasizes the need to stay dedicated to God and dependent on His Spirit for spiritual strength.

COMMENTARY

The final "judge" (or "deliverer" or "savior") recorded in Judges is a man named Samson. Hebrews 11:32 lists Samson among the heroes of faith, as one "whose weakness was turned to strength" (11:34). But the predominant picture of Samson in Judges 13–16 is of a man whose life was a one-man illustration of the plight of an entire nation.

As the story of Samson's life opens in chapter 13, Israel was again doing "evil in the eyes of the LORD" (13:1). As punishment, God again handed them over to their enemies, this time the Philistines. The Philistines had settled centuries before along the Mediterranean coast between Egypt and Gaza. They didn't much care for the Israelite occupation of Canaan, and they were in continual, though sporadic, conflict with God's people.

Samson's Potential (Judg. 13:2–5)

Samson's father, **Manoah**, was from **Zorah** (v. 2), located about fourteen miles west of Jerusalem in the foothills of the plains. Manoah's wife was **sterile and remained childless** (v. 2). Since children were considered a gift from God, to be childless was a sign of divine disfavor and disgrace. Like Sarah and Rebekah before her, and Hannah and Elizabeth after her, this desperate woman was visited by an angel of the Lord and comforted with the promise, **you are going to conceive and have a son** (v. 3). Whenever God had a special purpose for a man, there was generally something significant about his birth. This was the case with Isaac, Jacob, Moses, Samuel, Jeremiah, John the Baptist, Jesus . . . and Samson. Like Samuel and John the Baptist after him, Samson was to be **set apart to God from birth** (v. 5). He would be subject to the Nazirite vow for a lifetime (see 13:7), not for the voluntarily limited time specified in Numbers 6:1–12. As a Nazirite, he was to **drink no wine or other fermented drink** (Judg. 13:4), was to avoid eating **anything unclean** (as was the case with all the Israelites), to refrain from shaving his head, and to avoid coming in contact with a dead body. Notice in these verses, though, that his mother was to observe some of these stipulations as well, setting herself apart during her pregnancy, because she would carry no ordinary child. The angel foretold that **he will begin the deliverance of Israel from the hands of the Philistines** (v. 5). He would be God's instrument to save His people.

WORDS FROM WESLEY

Judges 13:5

A Nazarite—A person consecrated to God's service. *Begin to deliver*—And the deliverance shall be carried on and perfected by others, as it was by Eli, Samuel, and Saul; but especially by David. God choses to carry on His work gradually and by several hands. One lays the foundation of a good work, another builds, and perhaps a third brings forth the top stone. (ENOT)

It is hard to imagine a child with more promise and potential than Samson. He came from humble beginnings but his future was bright. His birth and future success were foretold by an angel. His parents sought wisdom in raising him (v. 8). "He grew and the LORD blessed him, and the Spirit of the LORD began to stir him" (vv. 24–25). Throughout Samson's life story, we see his supernatural, God-imparted strength. "The Spirit of the LORD came upon him in power" (14:6, 19; 15:14), enabling him to tear apart a lion with his bare hands (14:6), to strike down thirty Philistines singlehandedly (14:19), and to kill a thousand men with the jawbone of a donkey (15:15). He also caught three hundred foxes and tied their tails together, tore loose the doors of the city gate and carried them away, and freed himself from his enemies' ropes with ease. His strength was well known among the Israelites and among the Philistines whom he tormented. Some commentators believe the mythical stories of Hercules have their foundation in the life story of Samson, so many are the similarities.

In spite of Samson's great promise and potential, he, like the nation he represented, was deeply flawed. He fell in love with a Philistine woman, claiming "She's the right one for me" (14:3). Later, after his newly acquired wife had been killed by the Philistines, Samson visited a prostitute (16:1), then fell in love with another foreign woman named Delilah, who conspired with the Philistines to set a trap for him (16:4–5). At every turn, Samson treated his heritage and vow with contempt. He married outside his religion, which was strictly forbidden in the law. He touched a dead carcass, eating honey out of the lion's remains. He toyed with Delilah concerning the secret of his strength, eventually allowing her to cut off his hair (16:6–18). He proved himself to be vengeful and ruthless and immature. His whining in 15:18, "Must I now die of thirst?" is reminiscent of the groaning of the Israelites in the desert (Ex. 17:3). Though he possessed great physical strength, Samson was wanting in moral fortitude and wisdom.

Samson finally divulged the secret to his strength: "No razor has ever been used on my head . . . because I have been a Nazirite set apart to God since birth. If my head were shaved, my strength would leave me, and I would become as weak as any other man" (Judg. 16:17). And while he slept Delilah cut off his hair. Sad words are recorded in 16:20: "He awoke from his sleep and thought, 'I'll go out as before and shake myself free.' But he did not know that the LORD had left him." Samson was seized by the Philistines and his eyes were gouged out. He was led out to captivity in bronze shackles. It was a terrible end to a promising beginning.

Samson's Punishment (Judg. 16:23–25)

One of the primary deities of the Philistines was Dagon, some sort of a grain deity also worshiped by the Amorites. Some texts call Baal "the son of Dagon," and there were temples to this god in Gaza and Ashdod (1 Sam. 5:1–7). Here the Philistines offered sacrifices to Dagon and celebrated because **"Our god has delivered Samson, our enemy, into our hands"** (Judg. 16:23; also in v. 24). They mistakenly equated Samson's capture with the superiority of their god. So, not only did Samson bring his own life to ruin, but he also brought the name of the Lord into disrepute. In reality, Samson was suffering because he had failed to obey the Lord, not because of anything Dagon had done.

While they were in high spirits, they shouted, "Bring out Samson to entertain us." So they called Samson out of the prison, and he performed for them (v. 25). The once-heroic strongman had become an object of scorn and amusement. He performed for them, maybe through dancing to music. It was humiliating. And it was his own fault.

Sin has disastrous consequences. Though alluring at the moment, it eventually bites us and robs us of our dignity and honor. Sin seeks only to destroy, and its pleasures last but a short time. There is a terrible price to pay for sin. Samson lost everything. And yet, God was merciful.

The greatest expression of hope in Samson's story is found in 16:22: "But the hair on his head began to grow again after it had been shaved." God wasn't finished with Samson. Although his punishment was great, Samson's hope remained because of the greatness of his God.

WORDS FROM WESLEY

Judges 16:28

Samson called—This prayer was not an act of malice and revenge, but of faith and zeal for God, who was there publicly dishonoured; and justice, in vindicating the whole common-wealth of Israel, which was his duty, as he was judge. And God, who heareth not sinners, and would never use His omnipotence to gratify any man's malice, did manifest by the effect, that he accepted and owned his prayer as the dictate of his own Spirit. And that in this prayer he mentions only his personal injury, and not their indignities to God and his people, must be ascribed to that prudent care which he had, upon former occasions, of deriving the rage of the Philistines upon himself alone, and diverting it from the people. For which end I conceive this prayer was made with an audible voice, though he knew they would entertain it only with scorn and laughter. (ENOT)

Samson's Petition (Judg. 16:26–31)

After performing for his captors, Samson asked the servant leading him to put him where he could **lean against** the **pillars** of **the temple** (v. 26). It is possible that he was truly exhausted from his performance and simply desired to rest, but it is also possible he already had in mind what he planned to do, and he merely pretended to be tired in order to have an excuse to find

these support pillars. These were the two primary pillars supporting the weight of the temple. Verse 27 says **the temple was
crowded with men and women; all the rulers of the Philistines
were there, and on the roof were about three thousand men
and women**. The extra weight on the roof would have caused
considerable stress to the temple's support structure.

●

WORDS FROM WESLEY

Judges 16:30

Let me die—That is, I am content to die, so I can but contribute
to the vindication of God's glory, and the deliverance of God's people. This is no encouragement to those who wickedly murder themselves: for Samson did not desire, or procure his own death
voluntarily, but by mere necessity; he was by his office obliged to
seek the destruction of these enemies and blasphemers of God, and
oppressors of His people; which in these circumstances he could
not effect without his own death. Moreover, Samson did this by
Divine direction, as God's answer to his prayer manifests, and that
he might be a type of Christ, who by voluntarily undergoing death,
destroyed the enemies of God, and of his people. They died, just
when they were insulting over an Israelite, persecuting him whom
God had smitten. Nothing fills up the measure of the iniquity of
any person or people faster, than mocking or misusing the servants
of God, yea, tho' it is by their own folly, that they are brought low.
Those know not what they do, nor whom they affront, that make
sport with a good man. (ENOT)

For the first time since Samson's tragic downfall, he called
out to the Lord in prayer. He pled with God, **"O Sovereign LORD,
remember me. O God, please strengthen me just once more"**
(v. 28). His prayer was one of earnestness and humility. He had
finally realized that the secret to his strength was his relationship
with the Lord, not the length of his hair (for surely it had not
escaped his notice that his hair had grown back). His request to
be remembered expressed his desire to have his relationship with
God restored. This is a prayer of true repentance and submission

to God. Moral failure is tragic, but God is merciful when we return to Him. And so He was merciful to Samson here.

Samson reached toward the two central pillars on which the temple stood. . . . Then he pushed with all his might, and down came the temple (vv. 29–30). Samson was willing to die in order to kill these Philistines who had made a mockery of him and of God. Although he asked God to let him **get revenge on the Philistines for** his **two eyes** (v. 28), it's obvious that there was some noble intention to his request. Otherwise God would not have granted it. And so **he killed many more when he died than while he lived** (v. 30). The angel had foretold that he would "begin the deliverance of Israel from the hands of the Philistines" (13:5). And so he did.

WORDS FROM WESLEY

Judges 16:31

Buried—While the Philistines were under such grief, and consternation, that they had neither heart nor leisure to hinder them. (ENOT)

Samson's family took his body and **buried him . . . in the tomb of Manoah his father** (16:31), proving his honor had been restored. But it was a sad end to a life that could have been so much more. Samson **had led Israel twenty years** (v. 31), which means he was probably only about forty years old when he died. Samson proves that the choices we make can severely limit how God can use us. He is faithful and can still work through us, but we limit our potential by treating our relationship with God too casually. This is a study the entire nation of Israel had to learn. And it's one we still need today.

DISCUSSION

A nation may be overly confident in its stockpile of sophisticated weapons and numbers of well-trained, well-equipped military men and women, but a nation's greatest strength should lie in the Lord. Discuss what happens when self-reliance replaces confidence in the Lord.

1. Read Judges 13:2–5. How do you think Manoah's barren wife felt upon learning that she would give birth to one God would use to deliver Israel from the Philistines?

2. Israel's deliverer Samson, a Nazirite, became self-reliant after routing the Philistines on several occasions. This led to his capture by the Philistines. According to Judges 13:23, to whom did the Philistines credit this capture?

3. When a believer falls into sin and disgrace, why do unsaved people often rejoice?

4. Why would you agree or disagree that the Philistines intentionally insulted Jehovah by making sport of Samson during a celebration of their god Dagon?

5. Have you known a believer who became an object of derision because he or she fell into sin? How can you guard against a similar fate?

6. According to verse 28, Samson prayed for revenge. Do you think a prayer for revenge is justified today? If so, when?

7. How would you respond to the allegation that Samson used his restored strength to commit suicide?

PRAYER

Father, help us to live before You as You command. Show us where we fail, that we might not take it lightly. And thank You that You stand ready to forgive and help us when we return to You.

11

FAITHFULNESS REQUIRES COURAGE

Ruth 1:3–18

We have a clear choice: God or gods.

After withdrawing from the fellowship of a local church, many believers have experienced distress and heartache. A Christian who seeks a better life in the evil world system learns the hard way that he or she has chosen the wrong environment.

Life was hard at Bethlehem during a famine, but God's people lived there. By choosing to leave Bethlehem and move to pagan Moab, Elimelech jeopardized the faith and well-being of his wife Naomi and their two sons. He and the sons died in Moab, leaving Naomi widowed with two Moabite daughters-in-law.

This study shows the importance of making wise choices.

COMMENTARY

The book of Ruth is one of the most beautiful passages in the Old Testament. It is read annually in synagogues around the world. One fascinating detail about the book is that it is found in the Hebrew Bible immediately after the book of Proverbs. Since the book of Proverbs closes with the discourse on the virtuous woman in chapter 31, the inference might have been that Ruth was an example of what the virtuous woman would look like.

The setting for the book of Ruth is found in the first verse: "In the days when the judges ruled" (1:1). The time of the judges was a time of spiritual waywardness for the Israelite people. Sometimes they were on fire for the Lord, and then they would cool off and stray into worshiping foreign deities. They were sometimes spiritually hot, sometimes cold, and generally speaking, inconsistent. As long as they had a strong leader, they seemed to do alright. Whenever there was a change in leadership, they faltered.

The famine mentioned in Ruth 1:1 is generally thought to be judgment from God for their sin. Often the people of the Old Testament viewed natural calamities as punishment from the Almighty. Bethlehem literally means "house of bread." It is interesting that this family left the house of bread and went to Moab in search of provisions. This constituted turning their backs on God.

The family names are Elimelech, Naomi, Mahlon, and Kilion. Each of the names has significant meaning. Elimelech means "to whom God is King." Now we see the situation confounded because the man whose name represents loyalty to the Almighty set his sights on the land of another god. Elimelech proved to be a fair-weather follower of the Lord. When difficult times prevailed, he packed his bags and moved on. There are many people today who live similar spiritual lives. They serve God as long as times are good, but as soon as trouble comes their way they lose their religion and do their own thing. Naomi means "pleasant" or "gracious." It depicts her character very well as far as can be discerned from the text. Mahlon means "sickly" or "weak." This most likely describes Mahlon's health even from infancy. It could be that he was somewhat sick and weak physically as a child because he certainly died young. Kilion means "pining." Perhaps Kilion was a conscientious sort of fellow who was, like his brother, of frail constitution. He too died young.

Ephrathite (v. 2) is an old term used for the people who lived in Bethlehem; Bethlehem was located in the southern half of Israel known as Judah.

It is interesting that Elimelech chose to take his family to the country of Moab, because Moab was not necessarily a place that the Israelites regarded very highly. Interestingly enough, King David referred to Moab as his "washbasin" (Ps. 60:8) some years later, even though he had once left his parents there for safety when he was running from Saul (1 Sam. 22:3). Ruth was David's great-grandmother, so he probably left his parents there because of their bloodline and connections.

Moab was a land of people descended from Lot's incestuous relationship with his older daughter (Gen. 19:30–38). The Moabite people inhabited Israel during the time of the judges and ruled over them for about eighteen years (Judg. 3:12–14). Additionally, the Moabites mistreated the Israelites during their desert wanderings (Deut. 23:3–6), even calling for Balaam to invoke a curse on them. So, we ask ourselves, "Why in the world would Elimelech move to Moab?" Of all the places where he could move, why would he choose Moab? Perhaps he was so spiritually forlorn that he couldn't think straight. However, we see in the grand scheme of things, God was at work even in Elimelech's waywardness.

Three Widows in Moab (Ruth 1:3–5)

Elimelech died sometime after arriving in Moab. His death is viewed by many as a judgment from God for embracing foreign gods. Mahlon and Kilion, both married Moabite women. Mahlon married Ruth, and Kilion married Orpah. For some reason, after about ten years of living in Moab, both Mahlon and Kilion also died. Hence, there were now three widows.

WORDS FROM WESLEY

Ruth 1:5

Was left of her two sons, and her husband—Loss of children and widowhood are both come upon her. By whom shall she be comforted? It is God alone that is able to comfort those who are thus cast down. (ENOT)

Planning to Return to Judah (Ruth 1:6–7)

Naomi **heard . . . that the LORD had come to the aid of his people** (v. 6) and the famine was over. She felt like the best thing to do was to move back home where, she hoped, some family members would help take care of her in her old age. Naomi gathered her belongings and her two daughters-in-law, and they departed for the journey home to Bethlehem. Naomi felt an obligation to provide for the young widows. It was the custom of the day for childless widows to marry and have children from the deceased husband's brother. This was known as Levirate marriage.

●

WORDS FROM WESLEY

Ruth 1:8

Mother's house—Because daughters used to converse more frequently with their mothers, and to dwell in the same apartments with them, which then were distinct from those parts of the house where the men dwelt. *The dead*—With my sons, your husbands, while they lived. (ENOT)

Naomi's Concern for Orpah and Ruth (Ruth 1:8–10)

Naomi then had a change of heart and was moved with compassion for her two widowed daughters-in-law. She encouraged each of them to go back to their mother's home where their families could provide for them. She blessed them with the statement, **"May the LORD show kindness to you, as you have shown to your dead and to me"** (v. 8). She wanted them to **find rest in the home of another husband** (v. 9). They were young and had their whole lives before them; they should remarry. Naomi gave each of them a parting kiss and together **they wept** (v. 9). It must have been a moving sight along the dusty road to Judah—three widows weeping and talking and parting company. Both Orpah and Ruth expressed their desire to return to Judah with their mother-in-law.

They may have felt some obligation to help care for the woman who had given them their husbands.

Naomi's Feelings (Ruth 1:11–13)

Naomi eased the tension with a speech. She implored them to return home to their families and then addressed the matter of Levirate marriage. Naomi had no other sons, and even if she married that day and became pregnant that night, it would still be many years before the boys were old enough to fulfill the obligation to their deceased brothers by carrying on their family name. **"No,"** she said, **"It is more bitter for me . . . because the LORD's hand has gone out against me!"** (v. 13). Naomi felt that the reason all this calamity had come upon her was because of the Lord's judgment on her life. Sin does indeed have consequences. Naomi felt her life was bitter. She had great reason to feel that way. She was a widow who also had lost both children, and she was living in a foreign land with no relatives to care for her. Her plight was dire indeed.

WORDS FROM WESLEY

Ruth 1:14

Kissed—Departed from her with a kiss. Bad her farewell for ever. She loved Naomi; but she did not love her so well, as to quit her country for her sake. Thus many have a value for Christ, and yet come short of salvation by Him, because they cannot find in their hearts, to forsake other things for Him. They love Him, and yet leave Him, because they do not love Him enough, but love other things better. (ENOT)

Orpah and the Gods of Moab (Ruth 1:14–15)

After much weeping, Orpah parted with her mother-in-law and began the journey home to her family where she could mourn her loss and hopefully, remarry and start over. Orpah parted with a kiss good-bye. Yet **Ruth clung to her** mother-in-law (v. 14). She was more acutely attached and perhaps had a closer relationship with Naomi than Orpah did. Whatever the circumstances, Ruth refused to part ways and was determined to move to Judah and take care of her mother-in-law. Naomi again urged Ruth to go home like Orpah to her family and her gods. The prevailing god of Moab was Chemosh. Chemosh was a demanding god who, like Molech, required human sacrifice. The spiritual environment in Moab was dim and dark. Orpah went home, but Ruth had other plans.

WORDS FROM WESLEY

Ruth 1:15

To her gods—Those that forsake the communion of saints, will certainly break off their communion with God. This she saith, to try Ruth's sincerity and constancy, and that she might intimate to her, that if she went with her, she must embrace the true religion.

Ruth's Poetic and Exemplary Commitment (Ruth 1:16–18)

These are some of the most beautiful and poetic verses in the Old Testament. Ruth refused to leave Naomi and expressed her commitment to her and her God in memorable fashion: **"Where you go I will go, and where you stay I will stay. Your people will be my people and your God my God. Where you die I will die, and there I will be buried. May the LORD deal with me, be it every so severely, if anything but death separates you and me"** (vv. 16–17). Ruth hereby made a public commitment to both Naomi and the Lord. She vowed to be a part of Naomi's future whatever it took and embraced the God of Israel as her own. Her selflessness and religious fervency would be rewarded later, but for now, without knowing what was ahead,

Ruth's faith was exemplary. She was casting her lot with the Lord no matter what happened. She was no fair-weather follower of Jehovah like her former father-in-law. She was devoted to seeing matters through regardless of the consequences or circumstances. She walked into the unknown future with nothing but faith in Jehovah and an aging mother-in-law who would depend on her for survival.

It should be noted that all Ruth had to do to enter the kingdom of God was to embrace His covenant. She did not have to offer a human or animal sacrifice or perform any other type of religious ritual. She simply embraced the God of Israel with a heart of love and was accepted into His domain. Similarly today, in order to become a Christian, all you need to do is put your faith in the death and resurrection of Jesus Christ and repent. You cannot give enough money to the church to get the job done. You cannot get to heaven by doing good works. It is all by faith.

Naomi realized that Ruth was going to accompany her, so she stopped urging her to go home. In a way, this may have been comforting to Naomi. Her lot in life was bitter for sure; however, there was a little glimmer of sunshine found in the hope of better days in Judah and the presence of her daughter-in-law Ruth.

It is good to think for a few moments about the plight of these two widows. First of all, they were women in a male-dominated society. Women did not have the rights and status then as they do today in the West, although many women today still are mistreated simply because they are women. Second, they were widows. Their hearts were overflowing with the pangs of grief. Third, they were not able to work because women in those days typically stayed at home and took care of the household chores. There were few honorable ways for women to support themselves. Fourth, they were probably broke. Most likely, Elimelech sold out when he moved to Moab and whatever was left when he died was used up by Naomi in raising the boys. Fifth, they were childless. They had no descendants upon whom they could depend in their aged years. Society at that time had no Social Security or means for caring for the aged like the West does today.

Hard times were upon these two women and, without the help of their Lord, life would surely add misery to company. It is within this context that the remainder of the book unfolds the plan of God to care for these two women who were so committed to Him.

DISCUSSION

It may seem that trouble sometimes comes in bunches. Naomi's husband died and then her two sons died, leaving her a grieving widow and mother in a foreign land. Discuss what you would do in similar circumstances.

1. Do you think Elimelech and Naomi were right or wrong to leave Bethlehem and settle in Moab? Why?

2. How did things go from bad to worse for Naomi in Moab?

3. Naomi's sons married Moabite women. Do you think Christian parents should raise and educate their children where they are unlikely to fall in love with unbelievers? Why or why not?

4. As you read Ruth 1:6–18, what opinion of Naomi do you form?

5. What opinion of Orpah do you form?

6. What opinion of Ruth do you form?

7. What indication in these verses do you find that Naomi maintained a strong faith in the Lord through her trials?

8. How has the Lord brought you or someone you know through a time of deep sorrow?

PRAYER

Father, open our eyes to those around us who need our support, and show us how we can help them. In particular, give us opportunities to bless and assist widows, and so demonstrate Your love.

12

DO THE RIGHT THING

Ruth 3:1–11; 4:12–17

A God-directed life is its own reward, now and forever.

A little boy's sailboat stalled in the middle of a pond when a gentle breeze suddenly subsided. The boy felt he would never retrieve his boat. Then, an older boy picked up stones and threw them near the boat. At first the younger boy thought the older boy would destroy the stranded sailboat, but before long he realized each stone landed just beyond the boat and caused a ripple to form on the water. In turn, each ripple brought the sailboat closer to the shore, and eventually the little boy was reunited with his boat.

This study shows how God can use trials to draw us to himself and to work all things for our good and His purposes.

COMMENTARY

These passages contain the culmination of the story of Naomi and Ruth. All narratives in the Bible need to be studied as stories. In other words, we need to observe the main characters, the plot, and the scenes in order to correctly interpret the book. The story is named after Ruth, the daughter-in-law of Naomi, and in many ways the story is about both of them. This indicates that the plot revolves around these women. The men play supporting roles.

Every story plot has a structure that holds it together. *Pivot* and *chiasm* are especially common literary structures in the Bible. A narrative can change direction or "pivot" on a particular event. For example, the book of Numbers builds a sense of anticipation as the people prepare to enter the Promised Land; but it takes a turn toward despair after the people rebel in chapter 14.

"Chiasm" takes this change of direction further by repeating or matching a series of story components in reverse order after the pivot. The turnaround may involve repetition or paralleling of words, ideas, actions, or characters. For example, Jesus' parable about the lost sons in Luke 15 is built this way.

The plot of Ruth is structured with the same pattern. The book introduces Naomi along with her husband and two sons as a Jewish family living in Moab because of a famine in their home of Bethlehem (Ruth 1:1–2). Then Naomi's husband died and left her with two sons to raise (1:3). Her sons each married women from Moab; this was Ruth's entrance to the story (1:4). About ten years later, Naomi's sons died and left her with two daughters-in-law to support (1:5). Naomi heard from home that the famine was over, so she started to travel back—the pivot in this story's plot (1:6–7).

On the road home, she tried to send her daughters-in-law back to their families, but Ruth refused to go home (1:8–18). So the two main characters returned to Naomi's hometown of Bethlehem, where she told her friends to call her "Bitter" because of the pain she had experienced (1:19–21). Ruth and Naomi arrived in Bethlehem when the barley harvest was ready to be brought in, and Ruth volunteered to gather whatever grain the reapers left behind (1:22 – 2:2). She ended up gleaning in the fields of a wealthy relative of Naomi's husband. His name was Boaz, and he was also a well-respected man (2:1, 3). Boaz noticed Ruth and asked who she was. When he discovered she was Naomi's daughter-in-law, he arranged for her protection and for extra grain to be left behind for her (2:4–23).

This brings us to an important Old Testament tradition. Naomi thanked God for guiding Ruth into the field of Boaz, whom she called "one of our kinsman-redeemers" (2:20). In a culture without governmental assistance for widows, orphans, and others in poverty, the extended family was expected to care for them. The primary responsibility fell on the nearest male relative. The kinsman-redeemer's two main responsibilities were to retrieve and protect the family property of his near relative when it was offered for sale (Lev. 25:25–34; 27:9–33) and to marry the widow of a dead near relative in order to father children to the name of the dead (Deut. 25:5–10). The "close relative" would also be expected to purchase his kinsman's freedom from voluntary slavery resulting from poverty (Lev. 25:47–55). The "redeemer" might, in fact, avenge the blood of the dead relative if he found the murderer (Num. 35:9–28; Deut. 19:1–13; Josh. 20:2–9).

I Will Do What You Say (Ruth 3:1–6)

Once Ruth and Naomi made connections with Boaz, the restoration of their lives began to accelerate. **One day Naomi ... said to** Ruth, **"My daughter, should I not try to find a home for you, where you will be well provided for?"** (v. 1). Naomi wanted to provide security and rest for her loving daughter-in-law. If Ruth found a husband, he would care for both of them.

Naomi reminded Ruth that **Boaz** (v. 2), who had been treating her so kindly, was one of their kinsmen. Then she told Ruth how to ask him to fulfill his responsibilities as the kinsman-redeemer. She said, **"Tonight he will be winnowing barley on the threshing floor"** (v. 2). The threshing floor was a flat piece of land where the husks of the grain were broken so that the seeds could be removed. Winnowing involved gently tossing the seeds and husks into the air to separate them. It usually took place in the late afternoon when there was a breeze. Boaz and his men would stay at the threshing floor all night to guard the harvest from thieves.

Naomi continued, **"Wash and perfume yourself, and put on your best clothes. Then go down to the threshing floor,**

**but don't let him know you are there until he has finished
eating and drinking. When he lies down, note the place
where he is lying. Then go and uncover his feet and lie down.
He will tell you what to do"** (vv. 3–4). On the surface, this
seems a little seductive; however, this was a very appropriate way
for a widowed woman to seek help from her kinsman-redeemer.
It was in essence a marriage proposal, as we will see.

Ruth's response to Naomi revealed her deep love and respect
for her. She replied, **"I will do whatever you say"** (v. 5). And
Ruth did it. Her words matched her deeds. Ruth was fully
submissive and obedient to Naomi's instructions.

Wait for Him (Ruth 3:7–11)

Verse 6 says that Ruth "did everything her mother-in-law told
her to do," and these verses give us the details.

In the middle of the night something startled Boaz, so **he
turned and discovered a woman lying at his feet** (v. 8). In the
dark, he could not recognize who it was, so he asked, **"Who are
you?"** (v. 9).

Ruth identified herself and then said, **"Spread the corner of
your garment over me, since you are a kinsman-redeemer"**
(v. 9). This is the most sensitive point of the account, and the
most likely part to be misunderstood. The culture of the ancient
Middle East involved the practice of throwing part of a garment
over one being claimed for marriage (Ezek. 16:8). It did not
imply anything inappropriate.

WORDS FROM WESLEY

Ruth 3:9

Spread thy Skirt—That is, take me to be thy wife, and perform
the duty of an husband to me. (ENOT)

Boaz was impressed with Ruth once again, and he replied, **"The LORD bless you, my daughter** because **this kindness is greater than that which you showed earlier** (by caring for Naomi). **You have not run after the younger men, whether rich or poor. And now, my daughter, don't be afraid. I will do for you all you ask"** (vv. 10–11). Apparently Boaz had thought about his relationship with Ruth but expected her to seek out a younger man. The fact that the people of Bethlehem knew that Ruth was **a woman of noble character** (v. 11) implies that others had noticed her loving care for Naomi too.

●

WORDS FROM WESLEY

Ruth 3:10

Shewed kindness—Both to thy deceased husband, the continuance of whose name and memory thou seekest; and to thy mother-in-law, whose commands thou hast punctually obeyed. *Followedst not*—To seek thy marriage here, or in thy own country, as thou wouldst have done if thou hadst not preferred obedience to God's command, before pleasing thyself. (ENOT)

Boaz wanted to marry Ruth, but he knew there was another kinsman-redeemer who was a closer relative to Naomi. That man would have the first opportunity to fulfill the duties and to protect Ruth and Naomi. Boaz told Ruth to stay by him until it was light enough to return to town safely. So the next morning, Ruth reported all that had happened to her mother-in-law. Then Naomi said, "Wait, my daughter, until you find out what happens. For the man will not rest until the matter is settled today" (3:18).

Better Than Seven Sons (Ruth 4:12–17)

At the same time, Boaz went to the town gate (where legal transactions were conducted) and waited there. When the nearer kinsman-redeemer came along, Boaz asked him to sit and talk with him. Then Boaz asked ten of Bethlehem's leading men to join them as witnesses.

Then he told the kinsman-redeemer that Naomi was selling the piece of land that had belonged to her late husband, their relative. Boaz wanted to make sure this man had the opportunity to buy it first. When the closer relative decided he wanted to redeem the land, Boaz added one more concern. Boaz pointed out that as soon as he bought the land from Naomi and Ruth, he would need to marry one of them to keep the land in the name of Naomi's late husband.

At this, the kinsman-redeemer refused to buy the land because he thought it might endanger his own family's inheritance. It seems that the additional expense of providing for a wife, together with the prospect of losing the property if a son would possibly be born to the widow, caused the nearer kinsman to surrender his rights to Boaz. So they made the transfer of responsibility official in the sight of the town elders.

Then the elders and all those at the gate pronounced a blessing on Ruth and Boaz: "May the LORD make the woman who is coming into your home like Rachel and Leah, who together built up the house of Israel. May you have standing . . . and be famous in Bethlehem" (v. 11). Rachel and Leah were the two wives of Jacob who were the mothers, either naturally or through their maids, of the patriarchs of the twelve tribes of Israel.

The elders continued by praying that **through the offspring the LORD gives you by this young woman, may your family be like that of Perez, whom Tamar bore to Judah** (v. 12). Tamar was the widow of Judah's eldest son, and she ended up playing the part of a prostitute with her father-in-law in order to have a son to keep the family name going (Gen. 38). She gave birth to twins. One was named Perez, and he was an ancestor to Boaz (Ruth 4:18–22).

So Boaz took Ruth and she became his wife . . . and the LORD enabled her to conceive, and she gave birth to a son (v. 13). Ruth appears to have been barren while she was married to Naomi's son. When the baby was born, Naomi's friends and neighbors said, **"Praise be to the LORD, who this day has not left you without a kinsman-redeemer. May he** (the baby) **become famous throughout Israel! He will renew your life and sustain you in your old age. For your daughter-in-law, who loves you and who is better to you than seven sons, has given him birth"** (vv. 14–15).

WORDS FROM WESLEY

Ruth 4:13

Took Ruth—Which he might do, though she was a Moabite, because the prohibition against marrying such, is to be restrained to those who continue heathens; whereas Ruth was a sincere proselyte and convert to the God of Israel. Thus he that forsakes all for Christ, shall find more than all with him. (ENOT)

This book introduced Naomi as a widow with no sons to provide for her and living in a foreign land. It ends with God providing her with her loving daughter-in-law Ruth, and a new grandson in her hometown. As far as her friends were concerned, Naomi had a son because she took care of him as if he were her own. **They named him Obed. He was the father of Jesse, the father of David** (v. 17), who was the ancestor of Jesus Christ.

WORDS FROM WESLEY

Ruth 4:15

Thy life—That is, of the comfort of thy life. *Born him*—Or, hath born to him; that is, to thy kinsman a son. *Better than seven sons*—See how God sometimes makes up the want of those relations from whom we expected most comfort, in those from whom we expected least! The bonds of love prove stronger than those of nature. (ENOT)

DISCUSSION

Nearly everyone enjoys a love story. The story of what happened to Naomi's daughter-in-law Ruth in Bethlehem is an amazing love story.

1. How would you characterize Naomi based on your reading of Ruth 3:1–4?

2. What trait does Ruth reveal in response to Naomi's advice (vv. 5–6)?

3. Do you think Naomi and Ruth had a good mother-in-law/daughter-in-law relationship? Why or why not?

4. How do you know from verses 7–11 that Boaz was a God-fearing, righteous man?

5. If a young Christian woman asked you what kind of man she should marry, what would you tell her?

6. What do you find most uplifting about the "blessings" recorded in Ruth 4:12–5?

7. Compare verse 17 and Matthew 1:1, 5–6. What is the eternal sequel to the love story recorded in the book of Ruth?

PRAYER

Father, help us to grow into people with the integrity and Christlike heart that makes a good spouse. May we honor our (future or present) spouse and strengthen our (future or present) marriage by becoming more like You every day.

WORDS FROM WESLEY WORKS CITED

ENOT: Wesley, J. (1765). *Explanatory Notes upon the Old Testament* (Vol. 1–3). Bristol: William Pine.

PW: *The Poetical Works of John and Charles Wesley.* Edited by D. D. G. Osborn. 13 vols. London: Wesleyan-Methodist Conference Office, 1868.

OTHER BOOKS IN THE
WESLEY BIBLE STUDIES SERIES

Genesis
Exodus
Leviticus through Deuteronomy
Joshua through Ruth
1 Samuel through 2 Chronicles
Ezra through Esther
Job through Song of Songs
Isaiah
Jeremiah through Daniel
Hosea through Malachi
Matthew
Mark
Luke
John
Acts
Romans
1–2 Corinthians
Galatians through Colossians and Philemon
1–2 Thessalonians
1 Timothy through Titus
Hebrews
James
1–2 Peter and Jude
1–3 John
Revelation

Now Available in the Wesley Bible Studies Series

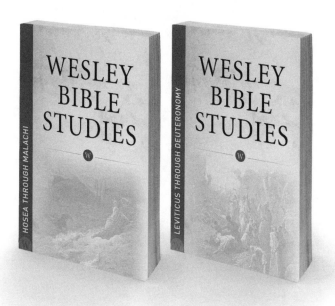

Each book in the Wesley Bible Studies series provides a thoughtful and powerful survey of key Scriptures in one or more biblical books. They combine accessible commentary from contemporary teachers, with relevantly highlighted direct quotes from the complete writings and life experiences of John Wesley, along with the poetry and hymns of his brother Charles. For each study, creative and engaging questions foster deeper fellowship and growth.

Hosea through Malachi
978-0-89827-852-1
978-0-89827-853-8 (e-book)

Leviticus through Deuteronomy
978-0-89827-858-3
978-0-89827-859-0 (e-book)

1.800.493.7539 wphstore.com